THE ART OF
THROWING

THE ART OF
THROWING

PRACTICAL INSTRUCTION FOR
BETTER TECHNIQUES

Amante P. Mariñas, Sr.

TUTTLE PUBLISHING
Tokyo • Rutland, Vermont • Singapore

Published by Tuttle Publishing, an imprint of Periplus Editions (HK) Ltd., with editorial offices at 364 Innovation Drive, North Clarendon, Vermont 05759 U.S.A.

Library of Congress Cataloging-in-Publication Data
Marinas, Amante P.
  The art of throwing : practical instruction for better techniques / Amante P. Mariñas, Sr. — 1st ed.
    p. cm.
  Includes bibliographical references.
  ISBN 0-8048-3787-2 (pbk.)
  1. Knife throwing. 2. Martial arts weapons. I. Title.
  GV1096.M26 2006
  796.8—dc22
                              2006035534

ISBN-10: 0-8048-3787-2
ISBN-13: 978-0-8048-3787-3

Distributed by

North America, Latin America & Europe
Tuttle Publishing
364 Innovation Drive
North Clarendon, VT 05759-9436 U.S.A.
Tel: 1 (802) 773-8930
Fax: 1 (802) 773-6993
info@tuttlepublishing.com
www.tuttlepublishing.com

Asia Pacific
Berkeley Books Pte. Ltd.
130 Joo Seng Road #06-01
Singapore 368357
Tel: (65) 6280-1330
Fax: (65) 6280-6290
inquiries@periplus.com.sg
www.periplus.com

First edition
11 10 09 08 07   10 9 8 7 6 5 4 3 2 1

Printed in the United States of America

TUTTLE PUBLISHING® is a registered trademark of Tuttle Publishing,
a division of Periplus Editions (HK) Ltd.

To my brothers and sisters Milagros, Ernesto, Patricia, Remigia, Pilar, Teodorico, Wilhelmina, Romulo, Manolo, and Marissa

In honor of my mother, Carolina Paclarin-Mariñas

In honor and in loving memory of my father, Virgilio Mariñas

In honor and in loving memory of my brother, Kuyang Pidiong, who helped me with my English when I was in grade school

Contents

Acknowledgments

I gave classes during weekends when I lived in Queens, New York. In one of my training sessions, I mentioned that I intended to write a book on knife throwing. A couple of weeks later, Spencer Gee gave me two books on the subject and tasseled Chinese throwing darts.

During water breaks, my students usually asked me what my current projects were. At one time, I told my class that I wanted to make a bagakay and a throwing disk but did not have any tools. Ueli Laeng came forward and asked if I could give him the specifications. I did and gave him wood for the bagakay, and thought nothing of it afterwards. A couple of weeks later, he came to class with several bagakays and disks. I did not know that he was a supervisor in a machine shop.

On one of my birthdays, a family friend gave me a mean-looking knife—the AK-47 bayonet. I teach knife fighting and I showed my class the bayonet and then mused aloud that I would have to do a lot of walking in the process of learning how to throw it. That year, sometime in November, I received a box with ten older versions of the AK-47 bayonet. That really made my Christmas. Thanks, John.

In 1997, I decided to move to Fredericksburg, Virginia. My students gave me a going-away party at Flushing Meadows Park—and presents. I got a book on the throwing of the shuriken and a camera from Spencer; a knife throwing book and two throwing axes/darts from Tracy Pearce, and a printer to replace my broken one, courtesy of several students who pooled their resources together.

Not long after I moved to Fredericksburg, a number of students from the surrounding area came to train with me. They are no less generous than my students in Queens.

Steve Charlson gave me knives and a pair of sais. I threw them—not away—but at cardboard targets.

In 1999, I designed a knife. At that time, I only knew how to make wooden knives. Peter Sampogna and Ueli fabricated the steel knives for me. One of the knives, the VM Bulalakaw, was marketed by United Cutlery.

One of my friends, Orlando Davidson, fabricated the first ax that I designed. Later, I designed and fabricated my throwing axes. I had only a hacksaw to cut the steel and in the process, I abused my hands. Tracy, Larry Schnitzer, and Rob Mulligan sent me rotary cutting tools to save my fingers.

A virus ruined my graphics software, and for some time, I had a problem making sketches for my manuscripts. Thoraya Zedan got an updated version of the software for me for a third of its market price. She later gave me a desktop and then a laptop computer to replace my old one. Thoraya also gave me a metal detector when I was having problems finding my throwing knives in the grass in my backyard.

I have students in Fredericksburg who went out of their way to bring me the very important cardboard boxes. Two of our family friends, Lina Chan and Francine Moore, would simply toss the cardboard over the fence and I had to make phone calls to find out whom to thank. Thoraya and Wayne Chenault brought me plywood. Wayne also loaned me his belt sander.

Anette Veldhuyzen took the photographs for the Methods of Throwing and Mechanics of the Throw sections of this book. Thoraya Zedan took all the other photographs. Anette also gave me western darts.

It took me about three years to complete the text of this work—but only because I am fortunate to have many generous friends and students. Without them, it would have taken me longer. I owe all a thousand thanks.

Books, knives, axes, wood, computers, cameras, and cardboard boxes were all essential in the completion of this work. The other important element was time. For this I must thank my sisters-in-law, Olivia Tan and Sylvia Chase, for the many hours that they have saved me.

I owe special thanks to my wife Cherry and my son Amante Jr. for giving me all the time I needed to write this book.

Preface

"The journey of a thousand miles starts with the first step." So the saying goes. But then, if you thought about how far *that* thousand miles is, compared to the length of one step, there is a good chance that you will never get there. One day, I sat down and estimated the distance I had covered throwing knives and other implements; I knew I had walked a lot, but I did not know how far. After some arithmetic, I calculated that I had traveled 1,600 miles.

I did not set out to walk 1,600 miles. I merely wanted to learn to throw a knife and hit the target. Indeed, my first goal was a modest one: I merely wanted to throw a knife ten times and experience how it feels.

I continued until I had thrown that knife 100 times. Even though I was missing more than hitting my target, it felt good. Then, I aimed to throw 500 times and achieved it. Modest goals, but they were significant steps. After that I became ambitious and set my sights at 1,000 throws.

I started hitting the bull's-eye, and, many times I called my son and my wife out to look at where I hit the target. Eventually, however, I had to stop calling them because I was hitting the bull's-eye very often, and it was taking too much time from my wife's and my son's work. Hitting the eye of my paper target became an ordinary occurrence.

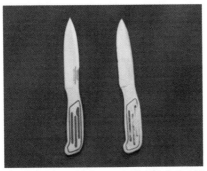

At right is the VM Bulalakaw I used for my millionth throw. I have thrown this particular knife about 100,000 times. At left is a brand new VM Bulalakaw. The initial VM is to honor the memory of my father. The VM Bulalakaw, a knife that I designed, was marketed by United Cutlery Corporation.

My next goal was to throw 10,000 times—which I did. I hit the ceiling of my basement in Queens, New York quite often in getting to that milestone. Then I set another goal: 50,000 throws. I was so elated when I reached this milestone that I cut away my circular target, placed it in transparent plastic, and kept it in a binder.

I kept on throwing. I also kept a daily log of my observations, my frustrations, and elation from the very first throw that I recorded. That later became the basis of my first book on knife throwing.

I started writing this work when I got past 600,000 throws. When I got to 921,000 throws, the book became not merely one on knife throwing but one on *the art of throwing*.

I now throw in Fredericksburg, in a backyard that is 50' wide and 100' deep. I have more freedom to try new throws and heavier implements. I spent more than 3,500 hours throwing knives and other implements in the course of completing this work. In the process, I used cardboard targets, which when stacked, would be about 120 stories high.

I did not aim to throw knives a million times. I merely wanted to throw ten times. As it turned out, my first ten throws were my "first step" in a very long journey. I have since thrown knives and other implements more than 1,300,000 times.

I still have the circular target I preserved in that binder. I look at it from time to time with eyes that have been operated on and with brows that have deeper furrows. Did I get older?

In the village where I grew up, there is a saying, "Only the water buffalo grows old."

Introduction

I threw about 500,000 times in my basement in New York City and was able to make most any knife stick on my target. Indeed, I even threw the Philippine *balisong* (butterfly knife) hitting at an average of 96 percent. With the bagakay, I was hitting even better—over 98 percent.

I felt I had reached the limit of my accuracy with the right-hand overhand throw. The only challenge it presented me was the use of a different throwing knife. Hence, I decided to learn other throws using different grips and different throwing methods.

My first month of throwing underhand with my right hand gripping the knife by its handle was quite frustrating. However, 40,000 throws later, I was hitting with an average of 97 percent. I was satisfied with this average. I decided to learn to throw underhand with my left hand, although I had my doubts. However, 40,000 throws later, I was hitting with an average of 97 percent. I asked myself, "What next?"

I teach knife fighting. One of the knives I train with is the AK-47 bayonet. The AK-47 bayonet or any army-type knife can be held in the forward grip where the fingers are wrapped around its thick and almost flat handle. It is the grip that would be used in hand-to-hand combat. So, I decided to learn to throw the AK-47 underhand using the hand-to-hand combat grip. (I do not envision carrying an AK-47 bayonet on my person. However, throwing the AK-47 bayonet presents a challenge in two ways: it is heavy and it is not designed to be thrown.)

I couldn't wait to become good at it. So I threw the AK-47 bayonet about 400 times a day. My right arm started to hurt. For this reason, I had to let up and reduce the number of my throws. However, that did not fit with my goal of throwing knives and other implements a million times. Hence, I decided to learn other throws with my left hand. I reasoned that if I threw with my left hand, I could give my right hand a rest.

Again, I couldn't wait to master my overhand left-hand throw. My left arm started to hurt. By this time, my right arm was feeling fine. Finally, I found a balance between achieving my goal and keeping my arms pain-free. I alternated between left- and right-hand throws and between overhand and underhand throws.

I was about to fall asleep one night when a thought occurred to me: There are two ways of holding the AK-47 bayonet in hand-to-hand combat. I am already throwing it in the forward hold. I got up, took my AK-47 bayonet, and held it the other way: in the ice-pick grip.

The next day, I started throwing the AK-47 bayonet in the ice-pick grip from 20 feet. I have not stopped throwing it since.

I am now throwing the ax and the bagakay using the same throwing methods I use with my knives.

To experience something new, I decided to study a selected number of the throwing implements and methods from the Japanese and Chinese martial arts.

I had many doubts about learning new throws, throwing new implements, and learning new grips. Most of the things I worried about did not happen. I found that seemingly difficult throws can be learned by simply trying. You can do it, too.

1

Basic Concepts

Nobody taught me how to throw a knife. I had to learn from my mistakes. You can, too. And I can help.

You need several basic things: a good knife (or other throwing implements), a safe area to throw the knife, time, and patience. Equipped with these basic things, you can learn to throw. All it takes is practice to hit the target consistently and accurately. But, of course, to become skilled, you will need to understand and learn the basic concepts of knife throwing.

These concepts are discussed in detail. They include:

1. Grips. In seminars and classes I have conducted on knife throwing, the most common first question is, "How do I hold the knife?"

2. Methods of throwing. Right-handers will throw naturally from over the right shoulder and left-handers from over the left shoulder. From this starting point, we will cover throwing overhand and underhand.

3. Mechanics of the throw. This section covers the step-by-step actions that make up the throw.

4. Spins and rotations. For years, my teaching approach had been, "As a beginning knife thrower, it is not necessary to know how many spins happen or how the knife rotates as it streaks toward the target. This is mental clutter." However, I have since found that an explanation of the spins and rotations of the throwing implement seems to have a reassuring effect on the beginning knife thrower.

5. Throwing and sticking distances. One of my students said, "I have the knife that you designed; I have a pretty big backyard. But how far should I be from the target?" Good question. This section covers that critical distance.

6. Targets. Most of my students initially say that they will set up a target made of wood. Then it's my turn to ask, "How far is your nearest neighbor?" You would not want to disturb your neighbor with the sound of the impact of a badly thrown knife on wood. I will cover what materials to use and how to make the best of your space.

7. Tracking your progress and learning curves. If you become serious about learning how to throw, you will want to keep track of your progress. The *learning curve* will give you a quantitative measure for your sticks and misses.

Throwing a knife or any pointed implement is fun if you are able to make it stick and hit the target you aim at. However, you will have to be prepared to experience a sort of emotional roller coaster. There will be many ups but more downs—initially. This emotional roller coaster ride can be made visible by keeping score, that is, by counting your sticks and misses and then generating your learning curve.

Initial efforts to learn a new throw, a new method of throwing, or throwing a new implement are at the same time exasperating and exhilarating. For example: The most difficult implement to throw in my experience is the Chinese flying dart (Figure 109). It has an odd shape, and you cannot grip it the way you would a knife.

In my first 100 throws of the flying dart, I was only able to make it stick four times. Not bad. My next 100 throws were twice as successful. I was able to make the dart stick eight times. I felt good. However, my next 100 throws were not any better.

On the sixth day, I was elated. I was able to stick the dart thirty times out of a hundred. But on the twelfth day, I had a downturn. I managed to stick the dart only eighteen times out of a hundred tries.

All knife throwers will experience these ups and downs. You might decide to stop throwing when it might seem that you are not improving. Don't. Eventually with practice, you will become consistent and accurate. However, let me warn you. Practice does not make perfect. It can only get you to the limit of your ability. In the language of mathematics—to your horizontal *asymptote*.

Despite this personal limit, you will find knife throwing fun, relaxing, and challenging done alone, in competition, or in the company of friends who share the same interest.

Grips

The grip for any throwing implement will depend on its design. For example, there is a marked difference between your grip on a spear and on a negishi-ryu shuriken.

Most throwing implements can be gripped by the blade or by the handle. However, this only indicates which part of the implement is gripped, not how the fingers are positioned. For example: Figures 1 and 2 are both blade grips. Yet, they are very different. Hence, we have to describe the initial position of the fingers (Figures 3–6).

HANDLE AND BLADE GRIPS

These are fairly obvious when used on a knife or on an ax where the handles are distinct. However, the definitions implied by these grips cannot be applied to other throwing implements such as the spear.

We do not associate a "handle" grip with a spear although we hold it in approximately the same place each time it is thrown. Neither do we normally associate a "handle" or a "blade" grip with a two-pointed throwing dart. We do not consider a two-pointed throwing dart to have a handle.

We can however associate a handle grip with a one-pointed dart such as the Japanese negishi-ryu shuriken. But we cannot do the same with the Chinese flying dart where you will be hard put to determine where the handle ends and the blade begins.

Any attempt to associate a handle or a blade grip with the multiple-pointed shaken will fail miserably. However, the use of the terms *handle* (where the sticking point is toward the front) or *blade* (where the sticking point is toward the thrower) grip is very useful for one-pointed throwing implements.

POSITIONS OF THE FINGERS

It is not adequate to describe a grip by stating that the implement is held by the blade or by the handle. The grip must be specified by noting the initial position of the fingers on the throwing implement. In this regard, the more common grips include:

1. Curled finger grip. The four fingers are curled and the thumb squeezes the implement on the opposite side.

2. Straight finger grip. The four fingers are held straight and the thumb squeezes the implement on the opposite side.

3. Wraparound grip. The fingers are wrapped around the handle of the implement with the thumb pressing on the index finger.

FIGURE 1. Blade grip.

FIGURE 2. Blade grip.

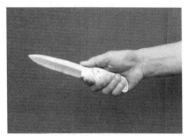

FIGURE 3. Curled finger grip.

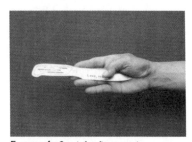

FIGURE 4. Straight finger grip.

FIGURE 5. Wraparound grip.

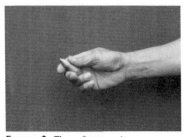

FIGURE 6. Three-finger grip.

4. Three-finger grip. The implement is held only with the index and middle fingers and the thumb.

5. Four-finger grip. The implement is held with the first three fingers and the thumb.

These and other unique grips are illustrated and discussed in more detail in later sections.

Methods of throwing

A knife can be thrown overhand or underhand. The overhand throw is the method most commonly used and written about.

I am right-handed, but I throw underhand and overhand with my left and right hands.

OVERHAND THROW

I throw the knife overhand in two different ways: from above my right shoulder (Figure 7) and from above my left shoulder (Figure 8).

There is more freedom of movement with a throw originating from above the same shoulder as the throwing hand. The knife can be thrown with its blade hitting the target vertically, diagonally, or horizontally. I do not throw the ax on a horizontal.

Your choice of throwing method can result from the throwing area available to you. For example: If you throw indoors such as in a basement with a low ceiling, you will have little headroom. To avoid putting holes in your ceiling, you will have to throw your knife overhand on a diagonal or on a horizontal—or by using the underhand throw.

A not-so-common overhand throw is the one that originates over the opposite shoulder as the throwing hand. I use this throw from 17 feet give or take a few inches.

UNDERHAND THROW

In the overhand throw, you can use your index finger or thumb as a pointer at the time you release the knife. In the underhand throw, this is not possible. You have to rely on feel as to when to release the knife. Perhaps it is this difference in the point of reference that makes knife throwers prefer to throw overhand; the "feel" for when to release the knife is not easily acquired. Indeed, it comes only after thousands of throws. Still, with practice, your underhand throw can become as accurate as your overhand throw.

I throw the knife underhand either from beside my right leg (Figure 9) or from beside my left hip (Figure 10). From beside my right leg, I throw the knife on a diagonal, on a horizontal, or on a near-vertical plane. Obviously, the underhand throw will be ideal when you throw small, light (at least 6 ounce) knives in a room with a low ceiling.

The underhand throw is not any more difficult to learn than the overhand throw. If you are already skilled in the overhand throw, you will be surprised at how quickly you will learn the underhand throw.

FIGURE 7. The overhand throw with the knife over the right shoulder.

FIGURE 8. The overhand throw with the knife over the left shoulder.

FIGURE 9. The underhand throw with the knife beside the right leg.

FIGURE 10. The underhand throw with the knife beside the left hip.

Mechanics of the throw

If you are a beginning knife thrower, you will first have to learn to throw the knife with enough speed to get it to the target. Then you have to learn to control the rotation of the knife so that it will get to the target point first.

To make the knife (or any throwing implement) get to the target point first every now and then is not difficult. However, for you to stick the knife consistently and accurately, you must throw it in the same consistent way in each throw. That is, the mechanics of the throw, the body and arm movements, must be nearly the same from one throw to the next.

The mechanics of a throw can be broken down into five stages: stance, the windup or the swing back, the swing forward, the release, and the follow-through.

STANCE

For a right-hand throw originating from the right side of the body, as a general rule, the left foot should be in front. For a right-hand throw originating from the left side, the right foot should be in front. This will allow for a body twist that will lend power to the throw and ensure a stable base.

The distance between the big toe of the rear foot and the heel of the front foot should be about $1^1/2$ times the length of your foot. If you do not find this comfortable, try a wider or a narrower distance.

The bend in the knee must also feel comfortable. It should be more pronounced for the underhand than in the overhand throw. This bend will allow you to raise your body weight in the underhand throw and to lower it in the overhand throw ensuring a powerful delivery of the knife.

The relative positions of your feet will depend on whether you are throwing overhand or underhand. When I throw overhand, my feet form an "L" that becomes a "V" at the completion of my throw. When I throw underhand, I set my feet in a "V" to allow my knife to clear my knee and to avoid putting a hole in my pants or cutting my leg. The "V" narrows at the completion of my throw.

Most knife throwers point the non-throwing arm at the target. I don't. As a carry-over from my stick-fighting training, I keep my non-throwing arm in front of my chest or at my side.

SWING BACK AND INHALE

Swing your arm back. At the same time, shift your body weight from your front to your rear foot. Inhale as you swing your arm back then hold your breath as you complete the movement. The backward swing should be smooth and not hurried.

In the overhand throw, do not pull your arm too far back, as this will cause your body to tilt backward. This will result in a subsequent forward motion that will be more like pushing the knife rather than throwing it. Merely twist your body as you pull your arm back.

In the underhand throw, swing your arm back like a pendulum. Do not swing the ax past the height of your hips. As a rule, stop your backward swing when you start feeling uncomfortable.

END OF THE BACKWARD SWING

For a knife that is a lot lighter than an ax, there is a momentary pause at the end of the backward swing. I throw a light ax overhand in the same way.

To throw a heavy ax, I swing my arm like a pendulum backward and downward at the side of my body. In a continuous counterclockwise circular motion, I bring it up above my shoulder, after which I start my forward swing. Because the $1/4$" VCM Palakol weighs over a pound, I cannot allow it to come to a dead stop. Hence, with the continuous circular backward then forward swing, I "slingshot" the ax toward the target (Figure 16).

FORWARD SWING AND HOLDING THE BREATH

The forward swing should be smooth. At the same time, you have to hold your breath. As the forward swing progresses, the weight of the body shifts to the front foot.

In the overhand throw, there is a slight swishing sound (as your arm and knife cut the air) toward the end of the forward swing and at the time of release. In the underhand throw, the arm swings forward like a pendulum.

RELEASE AND EXHALE

The knife must be held with just the right amount of "squeeze." If held too lightly, it will release early. If held too tightly, it will release late.

In the overhand throw, a premature release will cause the knife to sail over the target; a late release will cause the knife to hit the foot of the target. The reverse will result from early and late releases in the underhand throw.

The release of the knife must be by the "feel" imprinted on your subconscious through hundreds or thousands of throws. Indeed, the knife will release itself. The momentum of the knife will make it pull away on a tangent from the circular arc that your arm traces in its forward swing.

The release of the knife must be simultaneous with the completion of the shift of your body weight to the front foot and your exhale. You could liken the exhale to the kiai in karate or to the grunt in weightlifting. However, my exhale at the end of the knife throw is not as loud.

FOLLOW-THROUGH

Do not cut your forward swing short. The eyes must stay focused on the target until seconds after the knife hits.

In the overhand throw, the right (or left) hand should end at the height of the hip. In the underhand throw, the right (or left) hand should end at the height of the shoulder.

I place my (empty) left hand in front of my chest or at my side at the start of my right-hand throw. However, as the forward swing progresses, I swing my left hand backward to effect a powerful throw and keep my balance.

FACTORS THAT AFFECT THE MECHANICS OF THE THROW

The design of the handle will affect the timing of the release when you throw a knife by its handle. For example, a flared, knobbed, or long handle will delay the release. On the other hand, a tapered handle will speed up the release. A ventilated handle will provide a desirable drag and will enable the knife to stay longer in the hand.

FIGURE 11. The forward motion and follow-through in the right-hand overhand throw from over the right shoulder (A-B-C). If the knife is not released, the forward motion becomes a knife cut (A-B-D).

In a blade throw, the design of the blade will also affect the timing of the release. You will tend to release a narrow-bladed double-edged knife or a single-edged knife with a serrated back early. Nicks in your knife will make you open up your fingers prematurely.

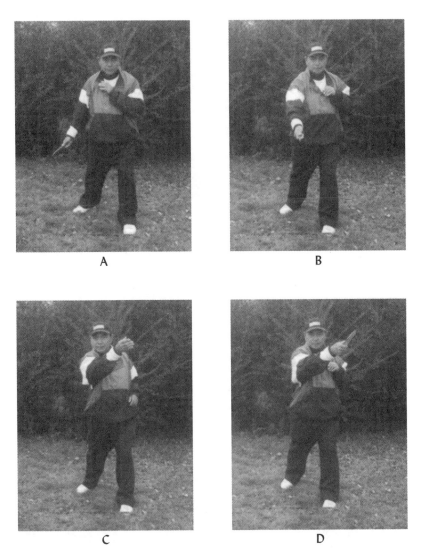

FIGURE 12. The forward motion and follow-through in the right-hand underhand throw from beside the right leg (A-B-C). If the knife is not released, the forward motion becomes a knife cut (A-B-D).

Be aware of details around you that will affect the mechanics of your swing. For example, baggy pants or an unzipped jacket will hinder your underhand forward swing, particularly on a windy day. Worse, if your elbow is bent too much, your knife could get caught in your jacket pocket. Even in the overhand throw, a flapping jacket will affect your forward swing.

| A | B | C |

FIGURE 13. The forward motion and the follow-through in the right-hand overhand throw from over the left shoulder.

| A | B | C |

FIGURE 14. The forward motion and the follow-through in the right-hand underhand throw from beside the left hip.

Figure 15. The windup in the right-hand overhand throw that I use on the $^3/_{16}"$ thick VCM Palakol. The follow-through is the same as that for the throwing of a knife.

Several other factors will affect the mechanics of your throw. These include:

1. Environmental conditions (sun, wind, temperature, bugs)

2. Mental clutter, such as fear of not sticking or of damaging the knife

3. Fatigue

4. Emotional stress

5. Trying too hard

6. Condition of your eyes

FIGURE 16. The windup in the right-hand overhand throw that I use on the heavier ¹/₄"
VCM Palakol. The follow-through is the same as that for the throwing of a knife.

Spins and rotations

As soon as you release the knife (or any throwing implement), it will spin end over end
around its center of gravity (CG) toward the target. If the knife is to stick, you must
control its rotation and spin such that it will hit the target point first. But how do you
control the spin and the rotation of a knife?

SPIN

You would have achieved control if the knife reaches the target point first after it spins 180° (half spin), 360° (one spin), 360° + 180° (1¹/₂ spin), and so on. Of course, depending on how you hold the knife and the distance you are throwing from, the knife might make the ¹/₂, 1, or 1¹/₂ spins and yet hit butt first. See Figure 17.

At this point, let me make a distinction between the spin and the rotation of the knife. Spin is defined in reference to the tip of the knife. Rotation on the other hand is in reference to the CG of the knife.

Several factors will determine the rate at which the knife will spin.

1. Bend in the wrist. There is a right time and a wrong time to bend the wrist. The right time is *after* the elbow has been straightened to the maximum comfortable limit. Bending the wrist at any other time will result in inconsistent if not inaccurate throws.

2. Relative distance of the index finger or thumb from the CG of the knife. The farther the CG of the knife is from the tip of your index finger, the faster the knife will spin. Thus, the ax thrown underhand gripped with the thumb about two inches from its CG (Figure 27B) will spin faster than the ax thrown underhand gripped with the thumb at its CG (Figure 27C).

3. Design of the handle. The knob of the handle of a knife such as the VM Bulalakaw (Figure 18, top) can catch on the heel of the palm or on the finger thereby giving it more pronounced spin. This will not happen if the knife has a smooth handle such as the CM Bituin (Figure 18, bottom).

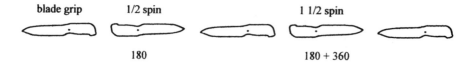

blade grip   1/2 spin   1 1/2 spin

180   180 + 360

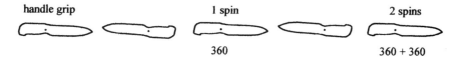

handle grip   1 spin   2 spins

360   360 + 360

FIGURE 17. For a knife to stick to the target, it must make half spins when thrown in the blade grip and full spins when thrown in the handle grip. In contrast, the two-pointed bagakay will stick whether it makes full (1, 2, . . .) or half (¹/₂, 1¹/₂, . . .) spins. Note that this diagram is not intended to indicate the knife's trajectory.

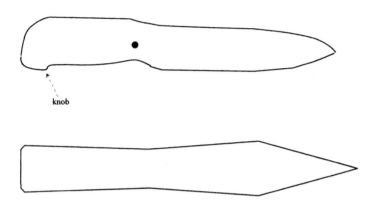

knob

FIGURE 18. The knob of the VM Bulalakaw (top) will catch on the heel of the palm, and that will give it a more pronounced spin than if a knife has a smooth handle (bottom).

Any knife or ax will spin clockwise if thrown overhand (Figures 19, 21); counterclockwise (Figures 20, 22) if thrown underhand. However, if the target is very close, it will seem not to. The knife could hit the target before its spin becomes noticeable.

The spin of some throwing implements can be suppressed but only at close distances. For example, I am able to suppress the spin of the Chinese flying dart when throwing it from 17 feet. I am able to do the same with the Japanese negishi-ryu shuriken when throwing it from 18 feet.

Heavy knives such as the Bowie can also be thrown underhand by the handle with "no" spin. The knife is simply shoveled toward the target. The "no" spin throw is ideal at point-blank range.

It is easier to leave the spin of the knife to the laws of physics. Instead of trying to control it, adjust to it. Step back to allow the knife to spin a few more degrees, or move forward to make the knife stick on the target before it spins a few more degrees.

The spins and rotations of other throwing implements are discussed and illustrated in later sections.

It is not necessary to know the number of spins a throwing implement makes to stick to the target. It can become mental clutter. For example: I throw with my right and left hands using different grips and different implements from different distances; I do not want to clutter my brain with the number of spins my knife makes for each of my throws. I do not have to know this when I throw my knife. When I teach, I do not tell my students to make the knife spin $1/2$, 1, $1^1/2$, times and so on. I merely tell them to either move back or step forward several inches at a time. Or, to give the knife a little more or a little less spin.

I make the beginning student throw (using the blade grip) from a distance such that the knife will make half spins because that way he can see how the knife will hit the target. Hence, it will be easier for him to make corrections on the throw. If a beginning knife thrower throws a knife with $1^1/2$ spins, he will not see how it impacts and will not

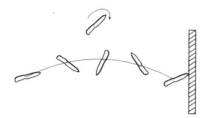

FIGURE 19. A knife will spin clockwise (viewed from the right side of the knife thrower) when thrown overhand.

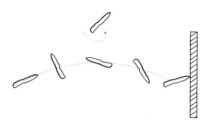

FIGURE 20. A knife will spin counterclockwise (viewed from the right side of the knife thrower) when thrown underhand.

FIGURE 21. An ax will spin clockwise (viewed from the right side of the ax thrower) when thrown overhand. This spin is transmitted to the ax by the clockwise rotation of the arm.

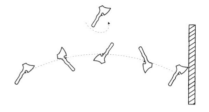

FIGURE 22. An ax will spin counterclockwise (viewed from the right side of the ax thrower) when thrown underhand. This spin is transmitted to the ax by the counterclockwise rotation of the arm.

be able to make corrections if it does not stick. Of course, if you do not have a teacher, you can ask a friend to observe how the knife hits.

ROTATION

The thrown knife will rotate around three mutually perpendicular axes: longitudinal, medial, and transverse (Figure 23). The design of its handle, the grip used, and the method of throwing will determine which rotation is more noticeable.

While the thrown knife can be made to rotate around any one of its axes, there is no such option with an ax. The ax will have to be made to rotate at its CG (Figure 24) around its medial axis (Figure 25). Otherwise, the result of the throw will be unpredictable.

Medial axis. The VM Bulalakaw or any knife thrown overhand by the handle in the curled finger handle grip (Figure 26A) or by the blade in the straight finger blade grip (Figure 26B) will rotate most noticeably on its medial axis and will have minimal rotation on the longitudinal axis.

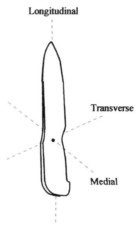

FIGURE 23. A thrown knife will rotate about its CG (shown as a dot) along three axes: longitudinal, medial, and transverse.

FIGURE 24. The CG of the VCM Palakol, shown as a dot (.), is outside its body.

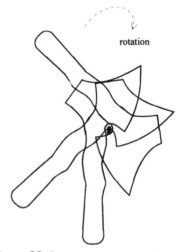

FIGURE 25. For an ax to stay on a true course, it has to rotate around its medial axis. This shows an ax rotating (on a plane parallel to the paper) around its medial axis.

| A. Curled finger handle grip in the overhand throw used on theVM Bulalakaw. | B. Straight finger blade grip in the overhand throw used on the VM Bulalakaw. | C. Curled finger handle grip in the underhand throw used on the VM Bulalakaw. |

D. Curled finger handle grip in the overhand throw used on the CM Bituin.

E. Ice-pick hold in the underhand throw used on an AK-47 bayonet.

FIGURE 26. Medial axis rotation. A knife can be made to rotate around its medial axis by using these grips. (A gymnast who cartwheels rotates around the medial axis.) The ice-pick grip can be used effectively only on a flat- and thick-handled knife such as the AK-47 bayonet. The ice-pick grip, used on a thin-handled knife, can only lead to inconsistent if not bad throws.

The VM Bulalakaw, which has a nonsymmetrical handle, when thrown underhand by the handle using the curled finger handle grip (Figure 26C) with the flat of its blade facing the ground can be made to rotate around its medial axis. The medial axis rotation is possible because as the knife is released the knob of the handle catches on the heel of the palm while the tapered top slides off smoothly.

A knife with a symmetrical handle, such as the CM Bituin, if thrown overhand by the handle using the curled finger handle grip (Figure 26D), will slide smoothly off the palm with neither the top nor the bottom part of the handle catching. Thrown in this manner the CM Bituin can be made to rotate around its medial axis.

The AK-47 bayonet will rotate around its medial axis when thrown underhand using the ice-pick hold (Figure 26E). Its weight and its thick handle will make it easy to throw the bayonet with little wobble.

It is neither logical nor practical to attempt to throw the VCM Palakol or any ax using any other grip than the curled finger handle grip (Figure 27). This is the only grip that can be used to throw the ax to make it rotate about its medial axis. Consider yourself lucky if you are able to make a wobbly ax stick to the target.

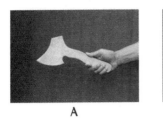
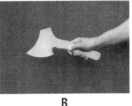
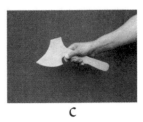

A   B   C

FIGURE 27. Medial axis rotation. An ax can be made to rotate around its medial axis by using this grip. Any wobble (rotation of an ax in its transverse axis) will result in inconsistent and inaccurate throws.

A. Curled finger handle grip in the underhand throw used on the VM Bulalakaw.

B. Wraparound handle grip (forward hold) in the underhand throw used on an AK-47 bayonet.

FIGURE 28. Longitudinal axis rotation. A knife can be made to rotate around its longitudinal axis by using these grips and turning the hand slightly over at the time of release. (A properly thrown football will rotate around its longitudinal axis. A figure skater's triple loop is a rotation around the longitudinal axis.) The wraparound handle grip can be used on either a thin- or thick-handled knife.

A. Curled finger blade grip in the overhand or under- hand throw used on the VM Bulalakaw.

B. Curled finger blade grip in the underhand throw used on the AK-47 bayonet.

C. Curled finger handle grip in the underhand throw used on the CM Bituin.

FIGURE 29. Transverse axis rotation. A knife can be made to rotate around its transverse axis by using the curled finger grip. (A gymnast who somersaults rotates around his transverse axis.)

Longitudinal axis. The VM Bulalakaw can be made to rotate around its longitudinal axis when thrown underhand using the curled finger handle grip (Figure 28A). At the time of release, I turn my hand over slightly to give the VM Bulalakaw a pronounced longitudinal axis rotation.

Similarly, the CM Bituin can be made to rotate on a pronounced longitudinal axis when thrown using the curled finger handle grip, by turning the hand over slightly at the time of release. The result is quite dramatic. The CM Bituin or any knife thrown in such a manner will corkscrew on its way to the target.

Transverse axis. A knife such as the CM Bituin, VM Bulalakaw, or AK-47 bayonet can be made to rotate on its transverse axis using the curled finger handle grip.

This grip can be used either on the blade (Figure 29A, Figure 29B) or on the handle (Figure 29C). Here, the knife is held with the flat of its blade facing the ground.

If you are able to give a knife a marked transverse axis rotation, it will head toward its target as though in slow motion.

CASE STUDIES

I have studied the rotations and spins of the bagakay, the AK-47 bayonet, and the VCM Palakol. Their different shapes make them interesting case studies in rotation and spin.

Bagakay. The cigar-shaped steel bagakay is a better throwing implement than a knife. Being two-pointed, it gives the thrower confidence that he can stick it. Hence, he can concentrate more on learning the mechanics of the throw rather than on worrying about hitting the target with the butt as is the case with a knife. After you become comfortable with the mechanics of the throw, learning to throw a knife will come easier.

The number of spins the 12³/₄" bagakay makes from different throwing distances using the grip as shown in Figure 48B are listed in Table 1.

TABLE 1. SPINS OF THE BAGAKAY.

Number of spins	Distance, feet
1	13
2	23
3	33.5

To identify which end of the bagakay sticks, I wrap a narrow strip of orange electrical tape on one end. I also wrap colored tape around its middle for easy location on grass.

AK-47 bayonet. The AK-47 bayonet was not designed to be thrown. However, it has excellent throwing characteristics. It is a versatile throwing weapon and can be thrown underhand and overhand using different grips on the handle and on the blade.

It is also sturdy. I have thrown each of the several used AK-47 bayonets I own more than 1,000 times, and there is still no movement in their bolsters. They were still as good as before. In contrast, the bolster of one other army-type knife became loose after only a hundred throws.

The most noticeable rotations of the AK-47 bayonet, using different grips, are summarized in Table 2. You can experiment with your throwing knife and generate a similar table.

TABLE 2. ROTATIONS OF THE AK-47 BAYONET.

Kind of throw	Grip	Most noticeable rotation axis
Underhand	Curled finger, handle	Medial
Underhand	Curled finger, blade	Transverse
Overhand	Straight finger, blade	Medial
Underhand	Forward hold, handle	Longitudinal
Underhand	Ice-pick hold, handle	Medial

VCM Palakol. The VCM Palakol or any ax can only be thrown correctly by making it rotate about its medial axis.

I have thrown the $1/4$" thick VCM Palakol as well as a lighter $3/16$" thick version both underhand and overhand using different placements of my thumb and index finger on its handle.

TABLE 3. SPINS OF THE VCM PALAKOL THROWN UNDERHAND AND OVERHAND.

Kind of throw	Curled finger handle grip	Number of spins	Distance, feet
Overhand	Figure 66	1	$21^1/_2$
Underhand	Figure 67	1	24

Throwing and sticking distances

For a knife or ax to stick to the target, it should be released from a given distance. This distance is called the *sticking distance*. This is to be differentiated from the distance of your front or rear foot to the target. It is important to know the difference.

The *throwing distance* is the distance from the tip of the toe of the lead foot to the target. The sticking distance is from the point of release of the knife to the target. Hence, the throwing distance is measured with respect to the foot while the sticking distance is measured with respect to the hand. The throwing distance is dependent on the length of the thrower's arm; sticking distance is not. To understand the difference more easily, consider two knife throwers: A who is 5'6" tall, and B who is 6'4". Each throws identical knives using the same blade grip.

A is able to stick her knife from a throwing distance of 18 feet with her knife making a full spin. With the given length of A's arm, she releases her knife at 16 feet. If 6'4" B throws the identical knife from 18 feet, he will not be able to make it stick. It will get to the target too soon. To make his knife stick, he has to move back because he has a longer arm.

Aside from the length of the arm, other factors could affect the throwing distance. These include:

1. Length of the knife. My throwing distance for a $6^1/_8$" knife using the straight finger blade grip is $17^1/_2$ feet. If I throw a 10" knife of identical design, I will have

to move back several inches to make it stick. If I do not want to move back, I have to adjust my grip on the knife or make adjustments in my throw.

2. Method of throwing. My throwing distance using identical grips on the VCM Palakol in an overhand throw is $21^1/_2$ feet; in an underhand throw, 24 feet.

3. Kind of grip used. My overhand throwing distance for the $8^3/_4$" VM Bulalakaw using the straight finger blade grip is about $17^1/_2$ feet; using the curled finger blade grip, 22 feet.

Angle of impact	Overhand throw	Underhand throw
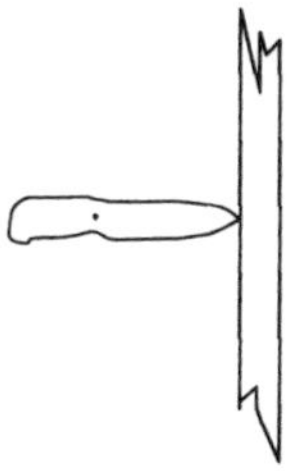 The knife hits perpendicular to the target.	Stay where you are.	Stay where you are.
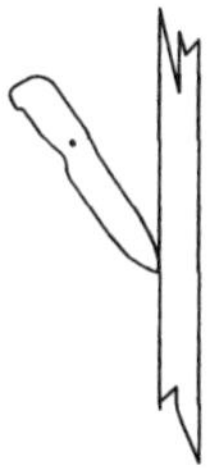 The knife hits with its tip down.	Step forward.	Step back.
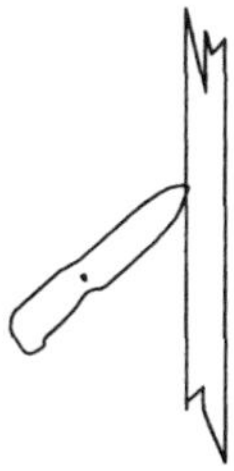 The knife hits with its tip up.	Step back.	Step forward.

FIGURE 30. Finding your throwing distance for overhand and underhand knife throws. When you make corrections, do not take big steps. Step forward or back a few inches at a time.

Overhand throw	Distance correction	Underhand throw
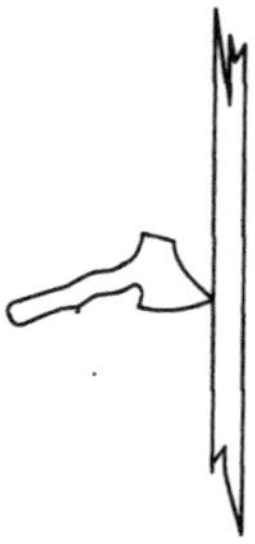 Tip of ax and its CG form a line that is perpendicular to the target face.	Stay where you are. Throwing distance is correct.	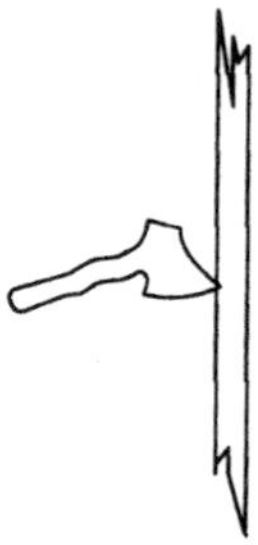 Tip of ax and its CG form a line that is perpendicular to the target face.
 Tip of ax points down.	Move closer to prevent the ax from over-rotating.	 Top of ax points up.
 Tip of ax points up.	Move back to allow the ax to rotate a few more degrees.	 Tip of ax points down.

FIGURE 31. Finding your throwing distance for overhand and underhand ax throws. When you make corrections, do not take big steps. Step forward or back a few inches at a time.

FIGURE 32. The VCM Palakol and the VM Bulalakaw embedded on a cardboard target that is backed by plywood.

If you do not yet know your throwing distance for a particular throw, grip, or knife, begin by throwing your knife from a range of 17 to 24 feet. If you are tall, start your throw from 24 feet. As you try to find your throwing distance, move half a foot at a time.

To find your throwing distance, observe how your knife hits the target. Point up? Point down? With the butt? Flat? Or just right? Figures 30 and 31 show the possible orientations of the knife (ax) and how to make corrections to find your throwing distance. If your knife (ax) hits with its butt, you can either step forward or step back.

Once you are able to determine your throwing distance for a particular knife (ax) using a particular grip and a particular throw, mark it by driving a short visible stake into or by drawing a line on the ground. From here on, you should be able to stick your knife (ax) with accuracy and consistency (Figure 32).

INCREASING YOUR THROWING DISTANCE

After being able to stick your knife consistently and accurately from a given distance using a particular grip, throw, and knife, you might want to throw from farther away. How do you determine the next farther distance?

You can use trial and error as you did when you were just starting to learn how to throw and start scratching your head all over again, or you can use a little algebra.

Recall earlier that I made a distinction between sticking distance and throwing distance. They are related by the equation

Throwing distance = Sticking distance + Arm reach

This relationship is shown in Figure 33.

FIGURE 33. Relationship between throwing and sticking distances. Arm reach is the distance between your front toe and the point of contact with the ground of a plumb line dropped from the tip of your index finger.

Arm reach will vary from one thrower to another. A thrower with longer arms will have a longer arm reach than one who has shorter arms.

A thrower's arm reach will become a constant, or nearly so, after the mechanics of a throw are committed to his neuromuscular memory (after many years of dedicated practice and thousands of throws). However, note that the thrower will stretch more to the front if the implement he is throwing is too heavy for him.

We can determine the next farther distance for a throw separately for blade and handle throws. The following calculations are based on a one-pointed knife—one with its center of gravity in the middle—thrown with a spin.

Handle throw. The knife can be thrown by the handle at point-blank range or shoveled at the target from some distance with apparently no spin. However, from a farther distance, the knife will spin before it hits the target.

The knife has to make full spins (1, 2, 3, . . .) if it is to stick on the target when thrown by the handle (Figure 17, bottom). Obviously, the closest distance you can be to the target in order for the thrown knife to stick in the handle throw is when it makes one full spin. We will call this your *first* throwing distance (Figure 34). We will assign the value X feet to your sticking distance. Thus,

$$\text{First throwing distance} = \text{X} + \text{Arm reach} \qquad \text{(Equation 1)}$$

To determine your arm reach, drop a straight line from your fingertips at the point you release your knife; then measure the distance to the tip of your front toe. Arm reach will normally be about $1\frac{1}{2}$ to 2 feet. We will use the lower value.

If you are able to make your knife stick from a throwing distance of 17 feet, your sticking distance is 17 - 1.5 = 15.5 feet. So X = 15.5 feet.

Your next (second) farther throwing distance for the handle throw will be 2X + 1.5 or

$$\text{Next (second) throwing distance} = 2(15.5) + 1.5 = 32.5 \text{ feet}$$

Hence, for the handle throw, Equation 1 becomes

$$\text{Throwing distance} = nX + \text{Arm reach} \qquad \text{(Equation 2)}$$

where n = 1, 2, 3 , . . . full spins or n = first, second, third, . . . throwing distance. The quantity nX is the sticking distance.

Spin can be suppressed if the implement is gripped with its CG in the palm. For example, I am able to throw the $5^5/_8$" negishi-ryu shuriken from 18 feet gripped with its point initially toward the target and make it stick with no spin. With this method of throwing, the shuriken behaves like a spear. I also use the no spin throw on the Chinese flying dart.

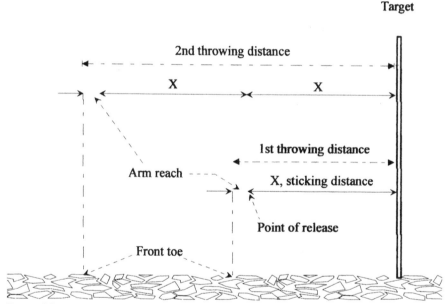

FIGURE 34. Throwing distances for the handle throw.

Blade throw. The knife has to make half spins ($^1/_2$, $1^1/_2$, $2^1/_2$, $3^1/_2$, . . .) if it is to stick when thrown by the blade (Figure 17, top). Obviously, the closest distance you can be to the target in order for you to make the knife stick in a blade throw is when it makes one half spin. We will call this your *first* throwing distance (Figure 35). We will assign the value Z feet to your sticking distance and 1.5 feet to your arm reach:

$$\text{First throwing distance} = Z + 1.5$$

where Z is the distance needed to allow the knife to make $^1/_2$ spin.

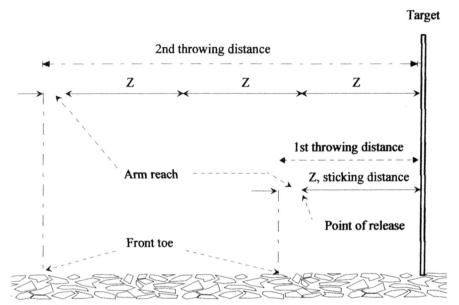

FIGURE 35. Throwing distances for the blade throw.

We will assume at this point that you are able to make your knife stick using the blade throw from 17 feet. This will make your blade throw sticking distance,

$$Z = 17 - 1.5 = 15.5 \text{ feet}$$

After the first one half spin, the knife will hit the target point first. If the knife is allowed to make another one half spin and there is a target at that point, it will hit butt first—not the desired result. So, if the knife is to stick from farther away, your next (second) throwing distance should allow the knife to make a third half spin. Thus, for the blade throw, your

$$\text{Next (second) throwing distance} = Z + 2Z + 1.5 \text{ or}$$

$$\text{Next (second) throwing distance} = 3Z + 1.5$$

In our particular example, your

$$\text{Next (second) throwing distance} = 3(15.5) + 1.5 = 48 \text{ feet}$$

which could be a bit too far for you; you will need to walk 96 feet to throw and retrieve your knife, which is good if you want to lose weight or could use the exercise.

In general, for the blade throw

$$\text{Throwing distance} = (2n + 1)Z + \text{Arm reach} \qquad \text{(Equation 3)}$$

where $(2n + 1)$ is the number of half spins and $n = 0, 1, 2, 3 \ldots$. The quantity $(2n + 1)Z$ is the sticking distance.

Your first throwing distance for the blade throw is when $n = 0$. In our example, when $n = 2$, you will have to throw from 79 feet.

You might try to get around these algebraic equations and shorten the distance of your knife throws by bending your wrist before your elbow reaches its maximum comfortable extension. Don't. This will result in inconsistent and inaccurate throws such that in one throw your knife could hit point first; in the next, it could hit butt first. Or it could hit flat.

A story about a bayonet throw during World War II as narrated by author Harry K. McEvoy gives us an interesting opportunity to use the throwing distance calculations.

Skeeter Vaughan was at the head of a 6-man patrol of the Moccasin Rangers assigned to take a German pillbox. But first, they needed to eliminate the sentry. Although it was already dark, their uniform could give them away because of snow on the ground.

Skeeter Vaughan was a full blooded Cherokee from California. Because of his great skill, he became a professional knife thrower when still a teenager. Hence, he was asked by his men to take out the sentry. He threw a 16" bayonet downhill, in the dark, and hit the German sentry on the base of the skull. The next morning the distance of the throw was measured. It was found to be 87 feet.*

I have assumed that the slope is 15 degrees, giving a horizontal throwing distance of about 85 feet. He used the blade throw. Most professional knife throwers throw from about 9 feet. At 5'8", his arm reach would be about 2 feet. It would be reasonable to assume a sticking distance of 9 feet because his bayonet is 16".

We can calculate the number of spins his bayonet made using Equation 3 for the blade throw. It came out to be 9 half spins or $4^{1}/_{2}$ full spins. That was some throw!

Targets

You will need a good target set up in a location where there will be minimum risk of injury to you or other people. If possible, locate your outdoor target so you can throw in the shade during summer.

When throwing indoors, damage to floors can be minimized by covering them with cardboard. You may want to top the cardboard with used carpet.

Avoid throwing knives that weigh more than 6 ounces indoors. Do not throw axes indoors.

TYPE OF MATERIAL

Styrofoam. You have a number of choices for your targets. You can try the Styrofoam target used in archery. This target is inexpensive if you throw only occasionally and if you use small, light knives. However, if you throw a lot, this target will quickly put a hole in your wallet. Also, if you throw heavy knives such as the AK-47 bayonet, you will use up the Styrofoam target in no time at all. Replacing Styrofoam targets gets even more expensive when you throw the much heavier ax.

---

*Harry K. McEvoy, *Knife & Tomahawk Throwing*, pp. 88–93, Charles E. Tuttle Company, Inc., 1988, Rutland, Vermont.

Wood. You can use wood for your target. It is relatively inexpensive. But, of course, the longevity of your wood target will still depend on the weights of the knives or axes you throw and also on how often and how many times you throw.

Throwing knives is normally a safe pastime. However, when your knife hits a wood target at an oblique angle, it can take a wild bounce, and you may be hit by the bouncing knife. In a garage or basement with limited room, it will not be easy to dodge such a projectile.

Even with your wood target set up outdoors, the possibility of getting hit by a bouncing knife still exists.

Cardboard. Cardboard is the ideal target if you throw knives indoors.

Cardboard sops up the energy of a badly thrown knife and causes the knife to fall harmlessly to the floor. Besides protecting your person, you will avoid breaking glass windows, mirrors, lights, or utility meters. Even outdoors, cardboard makes an ideal target.

I use cardboard in my backyard for a number of reasons. First, it does not cost anything. You can get it for free from your neighborhood stores. Second, the orientation of the knife (ax) gives me an idea of how the knife (ax) turned in flight. This is because dents caused by knife impacts, even if the knife does not stick, are visible on the cardboard, as would not have been the case with a wooden target. There you have to guess how the knife hit in order to find your throwing distance. This aspect of cardboard is particularly helpful when you are trying out a new throw. Third, the noise of a badly thrown knife (ax) is not a good thing to hear on a beautiful sunny afternoon when your neighbors are relaxing on their lawns.

I throw at least 300 times every day. If I make ten bad throws, that is ten knife-to-target impacts that I do not want to disturb my neighbors with. Even the knives that stick will generate dull thuds that can be bothersome to people who might not share your enthusiasm for throwing, so be aware of the impact your pastime can have on others nearby.

Preparing the Target

Mounting the target. The setup need not be elaborate. Figure 36 shows the dimensions and relative distances of the target support I use for my knife throws. The installed target is 6 feet tall (Figure 39) and costs less than $40. For this setup, you need two 4" x 3½" x 8' sections of landscape timber and six ½" x 3" x 4' sections of oak (or any hard wood).

Cut the landscape timber into 4-foot sections. Nail one ½" x 3" x 4' oak section on each side of the timber with a 1-foot overlap.

Dig three 1-foot-deep holes in the ground. Set the 4-foot sections in the holes then fill the holes with dirt. Use a tamper to compress the dirt. (There will be considerable movement of the timber when the soil becomes loose from rain.)

Attach the cardboard targets to the ½" x 3" x 4' wood using carpenter's clips. Use four or five layers of cardboard. You now have back-to-back targets.

You need back-to-back targets if you throw on grass. When the grass on one side thins, throw on the other side to give the thinned grass a chance to grow again.

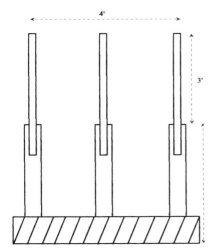

FIGURE 36. Dimensions and relative distances of the target support for my knife throws. I use a different setup for my ax throws (Figure 37, Figure 38).

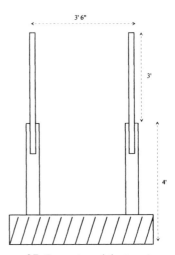

FIGURE 37. Front view of the target support I use for my ax throws showing relative distances and dimensions.

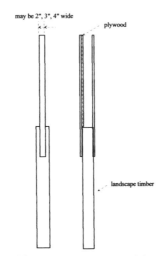

FIGURE 38. Front and side views of the target support for my ax throws. The thin darker layer is a section of plywood ($^{15}/_{32}$" thick, 44' wide, 36' high) to which I clip at least eight layers of cardboard.

FIGURE 39. Multiple targets for my knife throws mounted on the target support shown in Figure 36.

FIGURE 40. Installed target for my ax throws. The untidy looking hole-riddled cardboard at the foot of the target helps prevent dirt from getting on axes that hit point first but bounce off. Such an arrangement is even more important when the ground is wet.

The $1/4$" ax that I designed and fabricated weighs about a pound. Because it is heavy, it can easily put a big hole through several layers of cardboard. This will entail replacing the cardboard frequently. Indeed, after twenty ax throws, I have to replace the top cardboard because it gets mutilated. To somewhat reduce the size of the holes and to make the target last a few more throws, I use plywood as backing for at least eight layers of cardboard. The installed target (Figure 40) costs under $50.

Size of the target. When a knife is already embedded in the target, there is the possibility of the next thrown knife hitting it. If the knives you are throwing are all-metal, they will get nicked.

Knives with wood or plastic scales will suffer more damage. Their handles can get chipped or split by an incoming knife. This is very likely with knives such as the AK-47 bayonet, the handle of which is made of plastic that is $1 1/8$" at its thickest. The AK-47 bayonet is a relatively inexpensive knife—you can get a used one for under $20. Still, you want the AK-47 bayonet, or any knife you're throwing, to last as long as possible.

You will need a wide target to reduce the possibility of nicks and chips in your knives. Wide targets will allow you to throw several knives before there is a need to retrieve the already-embedded ones. A wide target is even more essential if you are a beginning knife thrower or if you are trying a new throw.

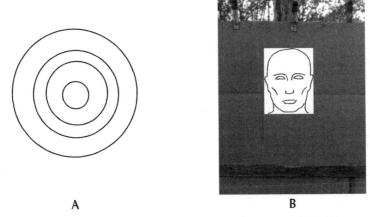

A   B

FIGURE 41. For sport knife throwing, I aim at a set of concentric circles (A). For defensive knife throwing, I aim at an outline of a human face (B). I use carpenter's glue to paste them onto my cardboard backboards.

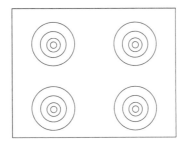

FIGURE 42. Multiple targets to reduce the possibility of knife-to-knife impacts.

For precision sport knife throwing, your target will necessarily be small. For example: I use a set of concentric circles (Figure 41A) printed on an 8^1/$_2$" x 11" sheet of white paper. For defensive knife throwing, my target is a human face (Figure 41B) printed on the same size paper. You can also use several sheets of 8^1/$_2$" x 11" paper on a wide field (Figure 42) to minimize the possibility of damage to your knives.

If you try to throw around the already embedded knife, you will start missing your target.

Tracking your progress and learning curves

If you throw knives only occasionally, you might be satisfied with merely sticking your knife every now and then. However, if you take knife throwing as a serious sport, you will not be satisfied with a few sticks. You will want to stick your knife more often than you miss.

If you throw on a daily basis and want to keep track of your progress, you need to record your hits and misses. Otherwise, you will not remember if you had more sticks today than a week ago. You can keep track of your progress in a simple yet effective way. Just count the number of times your knife sticks to the target then divide this number by the total number of your throws. Multiply this number by 100 to give you your sticking percentage.

LEARNING CURVES

You can make the calculations and generate a graph of your sticking percentage manually, or you can use a computer. Using a computer worksheet, you can tabulate your sticking percentage and generate a graph. Figure 43 is such a graph and shows my sticking percentage for months 1, 4, 12, and 15 for my left-hand underhand throw using the handle grip.

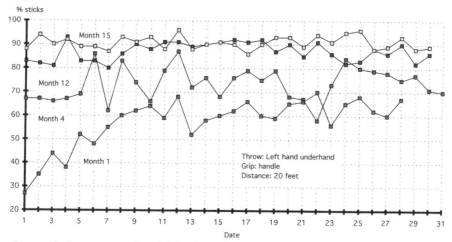

FIGURE 43. A comparison of my left-hand underhand throw using the handle grip in four different months.

The curve in month 1 is typical. I learned quickly, but I was erratic and inconsistent. I threw better in month 4, but I was still inconsistent. I had too many ups and downs; my hills were high and my valleys were deep. However, as I threw more (months 12 and 15), I was able to stick my knives more accurately and consistently. I still have peaks and valleys, but the variation is much smaller.

It is easier to keep track of your progress if you plot your *learning curve* after many more throws and over a longer period of time. For example: My learning curve for my left-hand underhand throw over a fifteen-month period is shown in Figure 44. This figure illustrates the typical shape of a learning curve. Learning comes quickly at first. For example, in the first month, the chart shows 57 percent sticks. This jumped to 70 percent in the following month. However, this rate of progress cannot continue indefinitely.

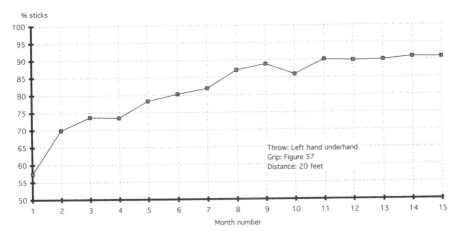

FIGURE 44. My learning curve over a period of fifteen months for my left-hand underhand throw. I am right-handed.

The learning curve is a limited growth curve—you cannot throw better than 100 percent. Eventually, you will reach the upper limit of your ability. For example, after month 11, my sticking percentage hovered in the low 90s. I still had a lot of room for improvement. However, I decided to learn other throws.

I have recorded all my sticks and misses and generated the associated learning curves for all my throws. Some of these are shown in later sections and can be used as benchmarks against which you can compare your progress.

How soon can you stick your knives consistently?

I record the number of throws of my students. However, at their request, I do not record all their sticks and misses. In one such case, one of my students threw 2,400 times before she felt comfortable enough for me to start keeping track. Her learning curve is shown in Figure 45.

The curve is steep in the first three months. (It would appear still steeper if I had recorded the sticks and misses from the very first throw.) The steep portion of the learning curve I call the *frustration zone*. This is where a beginning knife thrower could give up in frustration not knowing what she/he is doing wrong. In my students' case, I watch them throw, give encouragement, and make corrections on throwing distance, the mechanics of the throw, the grip, or mental focus. If a student throws too fast or too hard, she/he has lost focus.

In the fourth month, this student got over the hump and started sticking in the mid-80s. From this month on, she progressed at a smooth pace. In the eleventh month, she hit a high of 93 percent. For some reason, in the twelfth and thirteenth month, her average dipped. I have experienced similar dips in my throwing averages over the years; it often is due to mental clutter.

On average, in about six months and after about 10,000 throws, your technique will become consistent and will begin to enjoy throwing knives.

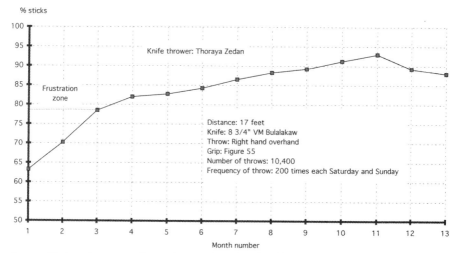

FIGURE 45. Learning curve of one of my students. It takes about fifteen minutes to throw one hundred times, that is, if you have ten knives. If you have fewer, it will take longer.

FACTORS THAT WILL AFFECT YOUR STICKING AVERAGE

Even after becoming skilled in throwing any implement, a number of factors will still affect your sticking average. These include:

1. Weight of throwing implement. For example, I am more accurate with a lighter ax than with a heavier one. I missed sticking the heavier 1/4" thick ax 163 times out of 4,500 throws. I missed sticking the lighter ax 31 times out of 12,800 throws.

2. Distance of the throw. You become less accurate as you begin to throw from farther away.

3. Type of implement. For example, you may be more accurate when throwing an ax than when throwing a knife.

4. Throwing hand. You will notice a difference between your right-hand and left-hand throws.

5. Method of throwing. You will be more accurate with one method than with another in the beginning.

6. Type of grip. You may find that you are more accurate with the forward hold than with the ice-pick hold.

Other factors, such as loss of concentration could affect your sticking average. For instance, if you've already hit the target ninety-eight straight times, missing could cross your mind—and very likely you will miss. Lapses in concentration can also be caused by physical distractions.

Distractions could take the form of a passing cloud covering the sun, a gust of wind, a siren blaring, or a squirrel in your peripheral vision. These factors could cause your throw to go awry, and they are all reflected in the learning curves.

It is not that difficult to throw an implement ten times and score a perfect ten. However, it is many times more difficult to throw fifty times and score a perfect fifty. It is even more difficult to score a perfect one hundred. For these reasons, I recommend throwing the implements in sets of fifty or one hundred.

To illustrate the difficulty of consistent sticks, I tabulated the frequency with which I came close to scoring fifty (hitting the target forty-nine out of fifty throws) and scoring a perfect fifty throwing the Chinese flying sticker. Since I threw the stickers in sets of fifty, it was not a problem grouping two consecutive sets of fifty throws into one set of one hundred throws.

TABLE 4. FREQUENCY OF PERFECT AND ALMOST-PERFECT SCORES FOR THE FLYING STICKER.
(Range of scores: 30–50 hits)

Score	Frequency, number of times
49	137
50	112
99	34
100	23

Since I threw the flying sticker fifty times a day over a period of 390 days (13 months), I had 390 chances of scoring perfect 50s. However, I was able to do so only 112 times. Scoring a perfect 100 is even more difficult. I had 195 chances but was able to do so only 23 times.

2

My Throwing Implements

All the throwing implements in this section are "mine" only because later in life I designed and fabricated them.

Many throwing implements are available in the market. However, I have chosen the bagakay (dart), VM Bulalakaw (knife), VCM Palakol (ax), and sibat (spear) to represent the most common throwing implements. Seemingly out of place in this section is the AK-47 bayonet, but because I throw it in a unique way, I have included it here.

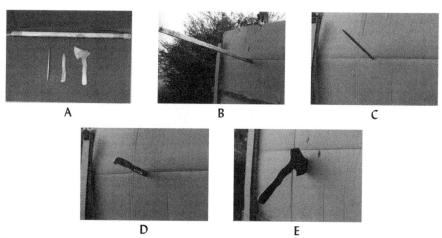

FIGURE 46. My throwing implements (A), spear (B), bagakay (C), VM Bulalakaw (D), and VCM Palakol (E) shown embedded on my cardboard target.

Bagakay

The bagakay was used by Filipinos to hunt birds for centuries before 1521, when the Philippines became a Spanish colony. There are historical accounts of the use of the bagakay to bring down birds from twenty paces (which is about thirty-five feet for the average-height Filipino), as well as its use against the Spanish colonists. In one instance of its use against the enemy, the bagakay was thrown with such violence that it pierced a Spanish soldier's armor and killed him.

The bagakay is a two-pointed (Figure 47) wooden dart. It can be made from hollow bamboo, which can be filled with clay to make it heavier and easier to throw. Obviously, any small branch of a tree can also be cut to the proper length, then sharpened at both ends to become an impromptu bagakay. It can then be fire-hardened to keep its point longer.

The wooden bagakay is a good throwing weapon despite its lightness. The bagakay is cigar-shaped but much thinner. The obvious way to make one is with a lathe. But you can also make do with a belt sander.

I rough-shape bagakays with a file, then give them a final finish on a belt sander. I have made 10-inch bagakays from oak, *bahi* (a Philippine palm wood), and steel.

One 10-inch bagakay that I fabricated from bahi weighs a mere 19 grams (0.68 ounces).

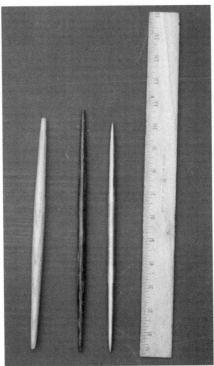

FIGURE 47. Two-pointed bagakays (l, r) made from oak, bahi, and steel.

GRIPPING A BAGAKAY

A bagakay is two-pointed, so it does not matter which end is gripped. The two grips I use on the bagakay are shown in Figure 48. The straight finger blade grip (Figure 48A) has limited use in close-quarter fighting. The curled finger blade grip (Figure 48B) is the more practical grip. I use both grips to throw the bagakay, but I have better control when I use the curled finger blade grip.

THROWING A BAGAKAY

Throw wooden bagakays overhand from over your right shoulder assuming you are right-handed. It requires a lot more effort to throw the light bagakay from over the left shoulder. I would advise against throwing a wooden bagakay underhand due to its lightness. I have thrown wooden bagakays from seventeen feet up to five at a time. So far, my best effort is to stick four out of five bagakays thrown simultaneously.

I throw the heavier steel bagakays from over my left and right shoulders, from beside my right leg and from beside my left hip.

The bagakay will stick on the target whether it makes half or full spins because it is two-pointed. However, the bagakay still has to be thrown from a given distance to make it stick.

Because bagakays are two-pointed, you cannot be too careful when you handle them. When you retrieve the bagakays, *first* pull out those that are embedded on the target. Any bagakays that fell on the ground should be retrieved *last*. This will prevent you from getting poked in the eye.

A. Straight finger
blade grip.   B. Curled finger blade grips.

FIGURE 48. The grips I use on a bagakay.

LEARNING CURVE CASE STUDY

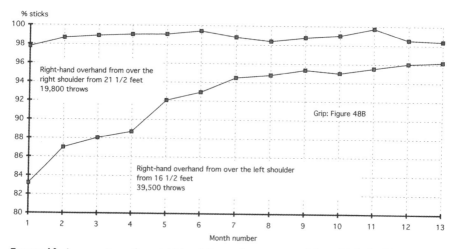

FIGURE 49. A comparison of my right hand throws from over my right and left shoulders.

Knife

Many throwing knives of different shapes, sizes, appearance, weights, and costs are available in the market. However, you will not find them all in one place. Even if you find five throwing knives pictured in a catalog or displayed on a store shelf, you will need certain guidelines to make an intelligent choice as to which knife to buy.

SELECTING A KNIFE

An intelligent choice can be made based on feel—the knife's weight and location of its center of gravity (CG), appearance—the shape of the blade and handle, overall length, which is directly related to weight, and cost. The interplay of these factors will determine the knife's throwing characteristics. These are listed in Table 5.

TABLE 5. FACTORS TO CONSIDER IN SELECTING A THROWING KNIFE.

Weight
Blade design and dimension
shape—leaf, diamond, clip point, spearpoint
width—narrow, wide
edge—double, single, dull
Handle design and dimension
flat, thin, thick
contoured to fit palm
even, tapered, flared, knobbed
Overall length
Cost

Weight. A knife will throw well if it weighs at least 4 to 6 ounces. This weight is particularly suited to throwing indoors. If your indoor practice room has a low ceiling, you will be better off with a 6-ounce knife that you can throw underhand. However, these knives will still leave pockmarks even if the floor is protected by a couple of layers of cardboard or carpet.

Outdoors, even 4-ounce knives can be pushed far enough by a 25 mph crosswind to cause you to miss your target. Of course, if you throw on grass or on bare ground, only your arm strength will limit the weight of the knife you can throw.

If you throw overhand, you will manage to make knives as light as 2 ounces stick on the target. But for the underhand throw, even 4-ounce knives are too light. Baseball, softball, and lacrosse players share the same experience. Consider Table 6.

Lacrosse and baseball use balls that weigh approximately 5 ounces. In both sports, the ball is thrown overhand. (In lacrosse, a pouched racket is used to hurl the ball.) Softball uses a heavier ball that weighs $6^1/4$–7 ounces. The softball is thrown underhand. Thus, there is a certain universality of throwing experiences among lacrosse, baseball, and softball players on one hand and knife throwers on the other. Heavier knives, and balls, are easier to throw underhand than the lighter ones.

TABLE 6. WEIGHTS OF SPORTS BALLS AND HOCKEY PUCKS.

Sport balls/hockey pucks	Weight, ounces
Golf ball	1.62 max.
Handball	2.3
Tennis	$2-2^{1}/_{2}$
Lacrosse	$5-5^{1}/_{2}$
Field hockey	$5^{1}/_{2}-5^{3}/_{4}$
Baseball	$5-5^{1}/_{4}$
Ice hockey	6
Softball	$6^{1}/_{4}-7$
Volleyball	9
Football	14–15
Soccer ball	14–18
Basketball	20–22

You cannot feel the weight of a knife unless you hold it in your hands, and if you are buying it from a catalog, this is not possible. However, you can use the dimensions of a knife to get an idea of how much it will weigh. For example: If a knife is 8 inches long and at least $^{1}/_{8}$-inch thick, it will weigh at least four ounces. I have seen only one catalog that listed the weights of its throwing knives.

Blade shape and dimension. The shape of the blade (Figure 50A–D) will not make one knife a better thrower than another. However, it can determine the grip on the knife.

If the blade is wide enough and single-edged, it can be thrown by the blade. If the knife has a wide blade or is double-edged, it has to be thrown by the handle. Knives with wide blades can pop out of the target even after sticking.

Throwing knives that are diamond-shaped (Figure 50A) or leaf-shaped (Figure 50B) are usually dull. If a knife is double-edged, it can be dulled by filing or by grinding.

The VM Bulalakaw is one-edged and has a drop point (Figure 50C) that curves away from the heel of the palm. Hence, when thrown by the blade, there is little risk of the point cutting into the palm. A knife with a clip point (Figure 50D) can also be thrown by the blade. However, I prefer to throw any knife with a clip point by the handle.

Handle shape and dimension. Handles (Figure 51) of throwing knives are designed to conform to the contour of the palm and to allow the same placement of the thumb and index finger from one throw to the next. For example: The in-line hilt (Figure 51A) and the off-line hilt (Figure 51B) allow the correct placement of the thumb and index finger for each throw. At the same time, the hilts serve as finger stops.

In contrast, the VM Bulalakaw (Figure 51C) is hilt-less. To ensure the correct grip, the thumb is placed on its sloping back at the same time that the little finger is pressed against its knob. The curved underside of its handle follows the contour of the closed palm.

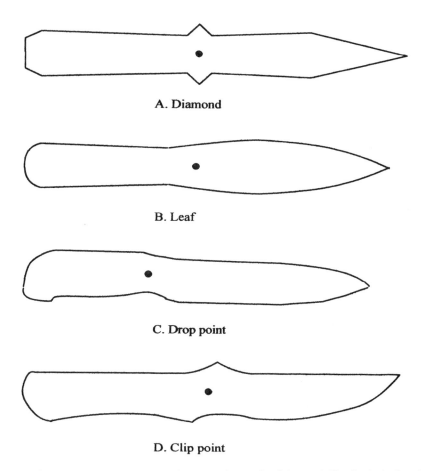

A. Diamond

B. Leaf

C. Drop point

D. Clip point

FIGURE 50. Different shapes of blades of throwing knives that I designed. The dot is the location of the knife's CG. (This and all other sketches are not drawn to scale.)

It will seem that the handle of the hilt-less hourglass (Figure 51D) does not allow for consistent grips. It does. The knife's handle will press against the heel of the palm. At the same time, the thumb and index finger are correctly placed at its narrow waist.

Not only the shape but also the length and thickness of the handle and the material it is made of have to be considered in the selection of a knife. Throwing knives that are $1/8$-inch thick could buckle when they make contact with a hard surface. The thicker $3/16$-inch knives can be thrown indefinitely without bending.

Avoid throwing knives that have wood or plastic scales since they can easily get damaged. Get all-metal throwing knives that have handles that are at least 4 inches long.

Overall length. It is easier to throw longer and heavier knives. A throwing knife with a 4-inch handle will have a total length of at least 8 inches. This is a good length for a throwing knife or for a knife designed for hand-to-hand combat.

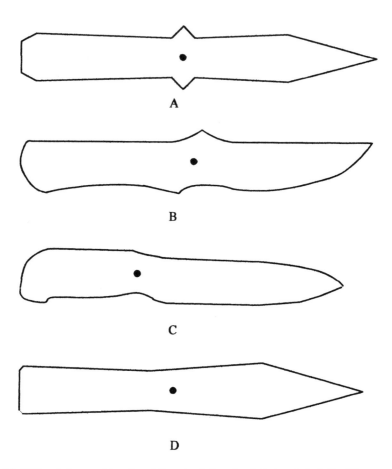

FIGURE 51. Different shapes of handles of throwing knives that I designed: A. In-line hilt, B. Off-line hilt, C. Hilt-less, and D. Hilt-less hourglass.

Cost. Most throwing knives are reasonably priced. A more expensive knife is not necessarily better for throwing. You would not want to nick an expensive knife. Any concern about a nick in your knife will become mental clutter and could cause your throw to err.

DESIGNING A KNIFE

A throwing knife must have heft. It must be heavy enough to feel good in the hands. A knife made of steel with the proper dimensions will give you the necessary heft. For example: A throwing knife made from a $3/16$-inch (thickness) by $1\frac{1}{8}$-inch (width) by 9 inches (length) steel plate will weigh about 244 grams or 8.7 ounces. The knife will weigh closer to 8 ounces because material will be removed to shape the handle and finished to give the knife a sharp edge. An 8-ounce knife will have enough heft and will stick with authority.

Obviously, if you want a heavier knife, you will either have to make it from a wider, longer or a thicker steel plate. However, a throwing knife can only be of a certain length and weight before it becomes impractical to carry it on your person.

I named my knife the VM Bulalakaw, VM to honor the memory of my father. When I was growing up, my father and I would look up at the moonlit night. From time to time we saw meteors. Bulalakaw, in my Philippine dialect, means meteor.

Length of the handle. Because I also teach the art of knife fighting, my goal was to design a knife that could be used for two requirements: throwing and fighting. My knife's handle had to allow for a quick release for knife throwing. At the same time, it also had to allow a secure grip for knife fighting. Unfortunately, these two factors are mutually exclusive.

I decided that this throwing knife must have a knob (Figure 52) to stop it from slipping through my fingers. The knob will not allow for a quick release. However, I rationalized that, if I wanted to give the knife a pronounced medial axis rotation, the knob is a desirable feature.

A knife must be fully in the grasp in hand-to-hand combat. Hence, including the knob, my knife has a 4-inch handle. (If you have big hands, the handle of your knife can be longer.)

I gave my knife a sloping back toward the front to ensure the same placement of the thumb for each throw. I also gave my knife a gradual downward slope at the back to give the heel of my palm a comfortable rest.

Center of gravity. I wanted the CG (Figure 50) of my knife to be, literally, at my fingertips. I located the CG of my knife in the handle to enable me to place my index finger (and thumb) over it in the handle throw. Thus, I decided that the CG of my knife must be at the 4-inch mark. I also wanted the CG to be close to the middle of the knife to enable me to place the tip of my index finger close to the CG in the blade throw.

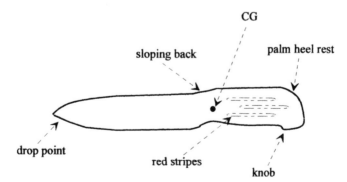

FIGURE 52. One of the knives that I designed. The VM Bulalakaw has a sloping back that ensures the same placement of the thumb for each throw, a knob that stops it from slipping through the fingers, and a gradual down slope on the back of the handle that allows the heel of the palm to rest comfortably on it. An added feature, the three red stripes on its handle, makes it easy to locate the knife in grass.

Length of the blade. A sharp knife will have a wedge-shaped blade. This will shave off some weight from the blade and will shift the knife's CG. To keep the CG where it is, the blade can be made a little longer than the handle, which will make the blade to handle length ratio slightly greater than one. A ratio of one means that the length of the blade is equal to the length of the handle.

The throwing knives that I have designed and fabricated have the following proportions.

$$1 < \frac{\text{blade length}}{\text{handle length}} < 1.24$$

This means that the blade to handle length ratio is greater than one but less than 1.24. Using the higher ratio, with a handle length of 4 inches, the length of the blade would be 4.96 inches. This gives the knife a total length of 9 inches.

A cursory glance at knife catalogs, and some arithmetic, will show you that most of the smaller throwing knives have blade to handle length ratios of less than one. The longer throwing knives have ratios greater than one. Army-type knives such as the AK-47 bayonet and the K-Bar have ratios that are, respectively, 1.24 and 1.03.

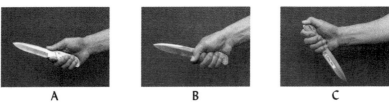

A   **B**   **C**

FIGURE 53. Hand-to-hand combat grip. The VM Bulalakaw can be gripped in three different ways for hand-to-hand combat: (A) with the thumb held on top of the handle, or (B) with the fingers wrapped around the handle in the forward, and (C) ice-pick holds.

You can compare this ratio to those of knives that are designed for cutting such as the *kukri* and the Philippines' *bolo,* which have long blades. Contrast this to folding knives where the handle is a lot longer than the blade.

GRIPPING A KNIFE

A knife can be gripped and thrown by the blade or by the handle. Which grip should you learn first? It's up to you; it's simply a matter of personal preference, and of the knife's properties.

Most knives that have leaf- or diamond-shaped blades are two-edged and have to be gripped and thrown by the handle. Even one-edged knives with serrated backs have to be thrown by the handle. Otherwise, the serration will cut the skin raw after repeated throws.

The one other factor that will determine where a knife should be gripped is the location of its center of gravity (CG). You want to feel a certain "heft" in the knife. If the knife is handle-heavy (its CG is at its handle), you will have a tendency to grip and throw it by the blade. If it is blade-heavy (its CG is at its blade), which is the case for most double-edged throwing knives, it feels better to grip and throw the knife by the handle.

Blade grip. You will feel most comfortable using the blade grip when its point does not touch your wrist. At the same time, the CG of the knife must be no more than a couple of inches away from the tip of your thumb or index finger. The closer the CG of the knife is to the tip of your thumb or index finger, the easier it is to control its rotation and spin.

The knife can be held using the *curled finger blade grip* (Figure 54) where the thumb is placed on the flat of the blade with the tips of the other three big fingers on the opposite side. In this grip, the thumb is used as the pointer, and the knife is thrown with its flat facing the ground.

The knife can also be held in the *straight finger blade grip* (Figure 55) where the thumb is held extended over the top of the blade. All the other fingers are straight and point to the front. The flat of the blade rests on the index and middle fingers, and the index finger functions as the pointer. Held in this manner, the knife can be thrown with the flat of its blade on a vertical, diagonal, or horizontal plane.

Handle grip. All throwing knives can be gripped and thrown by the handle. However, remember not to put the hilt or any part of the bolster on your palm. Otherwise, it could catch on the palm and will result in inconsistent and inaccurate throws.

Thick-handled knives such as the AK-47 bayonet or thin-handled knives such as the VM Bulalakaw can be thrown by the handle using the *curled finger handle grip*. In this grip, the thumb is placed on top of the handle with the tips of the other three big fingers on the opposite side. The edge of the knife can be oriented facing up, down (Figure 56), to the right (Figure 57), or to the left.

Thin- or thick-handled knives can also be thrown by the handle using the *wraparound grip*. Here, the fingers are wrapped around the handle with the thumb pressing

FIGURE 54. Curled finger blade grip on the VM Bulalakaw with its edge to the left.

FIGURE 55. Straight finger blade grip on the VM Bulalakaw.

FIGURE 56. Curled finger handle grip on the VM Bulalakaw with its edge down.

FIGURE 57. Curled finger handle grip on the VM Bulalakaw with its edge to the right.

on the index finger. Obviously, the wraparound grip cannot be used on knives with very short handles since part of the blade can become enclosed in the palm.

Held in the wraparound grip the knife can be thrown either with its point forward (*forward hold*) or with its point downward (*ice-pick hold*). The forward hold can be used on a thin-handled (Figure 53B) or on a thick-handled (Figure 58A) knife. The ice-pick hold (Figure 58B) can only be used with consistency and accuracy on thick-handled knives such as the K-Bar and the AK-47 bayonet.

A. Forward hold. B. Ice-pick hold.

FIGURE 58. The wraparound grips on an AK-47 bayonet.

Blade vs. handle grip. For the knife, gripping and throwing by the blade is as easy (or as difficult) as throwing by the handle. However, the latter is more practical.

Whether one grips and throws the knife by the handle or by the blade depends on the knife's design as well as on the time available for the throw. For example: Double-edged knives have to be gripped and thrown by the handle.

Army-type knives such as the K-Bar and the AK-47 bayonet have to be gripped and thrown by the handle for obvious reasons. Nobody fights hand-to-hand holding the knife by the blade. The need to throw the knife at any time, quickly, makes gripping and throwing army-type knives by the handle more practical. However, in a defensive situation and throwing from cover, there will be a time to grip the knife by the blade.

THROWING A KNIFE

A knife can be thrown from above the left or right shoulder, from hip level at the left side or from beside the right leg.

A knife can be given marked rotations about its longitudinal, medial, or transverse axes depending on the way it is gripped, the manner in which it is held, and the arm action. These are discussed in more detail in the section on spins and rotations.

Throwing a knife or any implement is basically safe—except for an occasional bad bounce, particularly when the target is wood. Using cardboard targets keeps you from having to duck a badly thrown knife.

There is one other potential source of injury in the underhand throw. Once, using the forward hold on the AK-47 bayonet, I managed to put a hole in my pants and a cut on my leg. Though the wound was superficial, it was thoroughly annoying. To avoid making the same mistake again, I had to angle the bayonet slightly to the right. As soon as my arm passes my right leg, I turn my hand over slightly to point the knife at the target.

LEARNING CURVE CASE STUDY

I became accurate with throwing the AK-47 bayonet using the forward hold rather quickly. Of course, all the other throws I made shortened my learning curve for this particular throw. It was not so for the underhand throw where I gripped the bayonet in the unusual ice-pick grip.

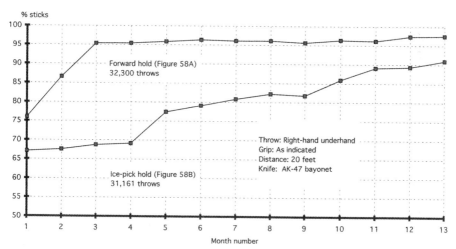

FIGURE 59. My learning curves for my underhand throw using the forward and ice-pick holds on an AK-47 bayonet.

I had an accuracy of about 67 percent in my first month of throwing underhand using the ice-pick hold compared to about 77 percent for the overhand throw. Attesting to the difficulty of throwing the AK-47 bayonet underhand using the ice-pick grip is the approximately 5 percent difference in sticking percentage in the thirteenth month.

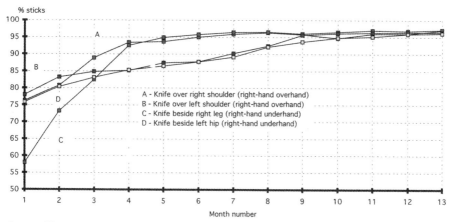

FIGURE 60. My learning curves for my right-hand throws from four different throwing positions (Figures 7–10).

Throwing with my right hand from four different positions. My sticking percentage, throwing with my right hand initially positioned over my left shoulder (B, Figure 8) and beside my left hip (D, Figure 10), are almost the same. But I got better quicker when I threw from my right side over my right shoulder (A, Figure 7) and from beside my right leg (C, Figure 9). Eventually after the ninth month, there is little difference between my sticking percentage from the four initial throwing positions.

After the thirteenth month, I felt I reached the limit of my throwing accuracy for these throws. At this point, I decided to learn other knife throws.

TRAJECTORY OF A THROWN KNIFE

Throw a knife some distance, observe its rotation, and compare it to that of a properly thrown football. The football will corkscrew, rotating smoothly around one axis, toward the receiver. On the other hand, a knife thrown into the air will rotate around three axes. Thus, the knife will seem to spin erratically.

The motion of the knife is not erratic. It is simply rotating about its *center of mass* (CM), the point in the knife about which its mass (*m*) is evenly distributed. Mass is not easily understood, but weight is so I use the more common term *center of gravity* (CG). The CG can be located by balancing the knife over a pencil or over your finger.

The CG of the thrown knife will follow a curved path the shape of which is determined by gravity and by air resistance. The thrown knife will become a projectile, and its CG will trace a *parabolic* curve called its *trajectory*. The trajectory of a knife does not depend on its weight.

We can locate a knife at any point in its trajectory (Figure 61).

Here the knife is released at an angle (A) to the horizontal and with its CG at point O. After traveling a distance of x feet, it hits the target.

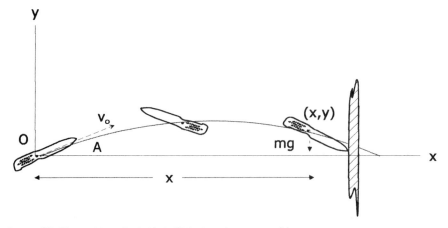

FIGURE 61. The position of a knife in flight (not drawn to scale).

The coordinates, the position of the knife, at any time are shown as (x, y). The x-coordinate, in terms of the time of flight t is

$$x = (v_o \cos A)t \qquad \text{(Equation 4)}$$

and the y-coordinate is

$$y = (v_o \sin A)t - \tfrac{1}{2}gt^2. \qquad \text{(Equation 5)}$$

Solving for t in Equation 4 then substituting it into Equation 5 yields

$$y = x\tan A - \frac{g}{2v_o^2 \cos^2 A} x^2 \qquad \text{(Equation 6)}$$

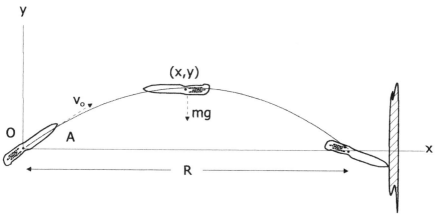

FIGURE 62. The special case where y = 0, x = R, where R is the *range*. (Not drawn to scale.)

In the special case where y = 0 (Figure 62),

$$x = R = \frac{v_o^2}{g} \sin 2A \qquad \text{(Equation 7)}$$

The maximum height the knife can get to is

$$h = \frac{v_o^2 \sin^2 A}{2g} \qquad \text{(Equation 8)}$$

The quantities x and R are related to the sticking distance (Equation 2, page 25 and Equation 3, page 26), that is,

Sticking distance =
x (or R) + horizontal distance from the CG to the tip of the knife

Ax

SELECTING AN AX

There are a limited number of commercially available throwing axes (tomahawks). Should you want to start throwing an ax, buy the first one you see as most of them have wooden handles, are single-headed, and throw equally well. I own several commercial single-headed steel axes of identical design. I would not recommend this for beginning ax throwers.

DESIGNING MY AX

Most axes (tomahawks) that are commercially sold have wooden handles. A throwing ax (tomahawk) with a wooden handle will not last indefinitely. Eventually, the handle will become loose or will break, and this is very likely to happen early on when you are just starting to learn how to throw the ax (tomahawk).

I wanted an ax that I could throw as soon as I got it out of the box, without having to modify it. I also wanted an ax that could withstand frequent and prolonged use. This kind of ax is not commercially available, so I decided to design and fabricate my own, based on the following criteria:

1. Its handle must allow a comfortable grip when the ax is used as a cutting tool, a secure grip when used as a fighting tool, and a quick-release grip when used as a throwing tool.

2. It must be heavy enough to cut wood with ease, to ensure deep penetration when thrown, and to inflict deep puncture wounds in hand-to-hand combat.

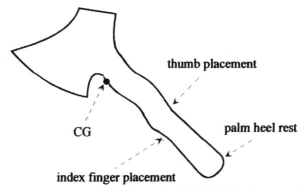

FIGURE 63. The ax that I designed and fabricated, the VCM Palakol, has an undulating handle that ensures the proper placement of the thumb and the index finger for each throw. The shape of the upper edge and the sharp angle of its point maximize the possibility of the ax sticking to the target both in the underhand and overhand throws.

I scoured the hardware stores in my neighborhood and found a 1' x 1' x ¼" steel plate that cost about $25. I traced my ax design on the ¼-inch steel plate and was able to squeeze in three axes. There was even enough steel left for two knives.

It was not easy making the axes. I only had a hacksaw to cut them with and went through three cutting blades. Straight cuts were difficult enough; the curves took the most time and the most effort. I used a combination of a rough file, bench grinder, belt sander, and a Dremel attachment to rough-shape, smooth, and sharpen the axes. Two months later, I finished the axes and couldn't wait to throw them.

I had no problem throwing the ¼-inch thick ax underhand. However, it turned out to be too heavy for me in the overhand throw. For this reason, I looked for thinner steel plates, found ³/₁₆-inch thick steel plates at a welding shop, and fabricated a lighter ax using the same technique.

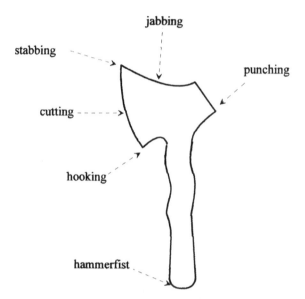

FIGURE 64. For hand-to-hand combat, the VCM Palakol can be used for jabbing, cutting, or stabbing. It can also be used for puncturing or as a fist load for delivering a hammerfist.

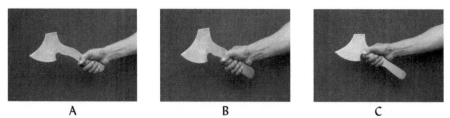

A   B   C

FIGURE 65. Hand-to-hand combat grips. The VCM Palakol can be gripped in three different ways for hand-to-hand combat. These grips can also be used for cutting wood.

GRIPPING AN AX

There are a limited number of grips you can use on an ax. Unlike a knife, which can be thrown by the blade, you cannot grip an ax by its head for throwing. An ax can only be thrown by gripping its handle.

The curled finger handle grip used on the ax in the overhand throw is shown in Figure 66. Here, the thumb is held on top of the handle just before the hump. At the same time, the index finger is placed just before the hump under the handle. This prevents the thumb and the index finger from being placed too far forward. The bottom of the handle presses comfortably against the heel of the palm.

The curled finger handle grip can be used on the ax in a unique way (Figure 67A) where the thumb and index finger are held at its CG. The index finger is placed close to the throat of the ax while the other three fingers are placed at the concave portion on the underside of the handle. The ax can also be held with the thumb and index finger a couple of inches away from the CG (Figure 67B).

FIGURE 66. The curled finger handle grip on the VCM Palakol (in the overhand throw) where the thumb is held about two inches from its CG.

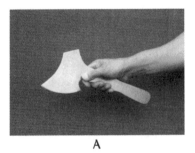 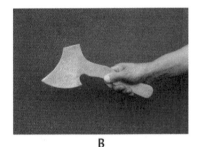

A   B

FIGURE 67. The curled finger handle grips on the VCM Palakol in the underhand throw.

THROWING AN AX

An ax may be thrown overhand or underhand. Thrown underhand, both the swing back and the swing forward must imitate the swing of a pendulum in one plane. Any deviation from a pendulum-like forward swing will result in an ax that will wobble toward the target.

A properly thrown ax will spin end over end and rotate only about its medial axis. An ax that wobbles could hit the target with its side and not with its point.

The ax impacts the target as it rotates downward. As a result, it pulls down the cardboard. For this reason, you might find it useful to nail the cardboard to the plywood backing at the top. (I drive in the nail just deep enough to pierce through the eight layers of cardboard and bite slightly into the plywood.) Expect to replace the first four layers of cardboard after about twenty throws because they become mutilated.

I did not make the point of my ax too sharp because I wanted the plywood backing to last as long as possible. Still, after 5,000 overhand throws, I had to turn the plywood so I could throw at a still hole-free part. By adjusting the placement of the plywood, I managed to make two panels last for 17,300 overhand throws.

It takes about twenty minutes to throw an ax one hundred times, sometimes longer.

LEARNING CURVE CASE STUDY

It will seem that I became very accurate throwing the ax very quickly. Not really. I still had to go through the frustration zone.

I started to throw the ax much later than the knife. However, there is no difference in the mechanics of throwing a knife and an ax. Hence, while I was throwing a knife, I was actually learning the mechanics of throwing an ax. Thus, my learning curve for the ax throw was shortened. This accounts for my high sticking average (Figure 68) right from the beginning.

My sticking average for the overhand ax throw is better than 99 percent. My sticking average for the underhand ax throw is about 10 percent lower. It is easier to make the ax rotate around its medial axis in the overhand throw than in the underhand throw. The ax tends to wobble more in the underhand throw.

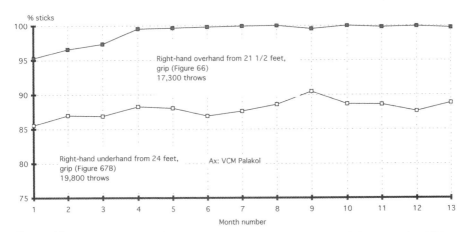

FIGURE 68. My learning curves for my right-hand underhand and overhand throws on the VCM Palakol.

The weight of a throwing knife or ax could affect your sticking average. For example: In the first three months, I used the heavy VCM Palakol. In month 3, I averaged about 97 percent. In the fourth month, I started using another VCM Palakol that was 25 percent lighter. With a lighter VCM Palakol, my average went up to better than 99 percent.

I missed sticking the heavier VCM Palakol 163 times out of 4,500 overhand throws. I missed sticking the lighter VCM Palakol 31 times out of 12,800 overhand throws.

Spear

SELECTING A SPEAR

A spear can be all steel with its point being an integral part of the shaft. This type of spear can be heavy; hence, it can be as short as 24 inches. However, a short spear will tend to rotate faster about its center of gravity than a longer spear and will require more skill to throw.

A spear can also be made completely from wood with its point hardened in a fire. A wooden spear will lose its sharpness when thrown repeatedly. However, it has the advantage of being light, so can be made longer, which will make it easier to throw. Also a wooden spear dulled by repeated throws or one that gets lost after a throw can be easily replaced.

The most common spear is one with a wooden shaft topped by a steel point (Figure 69). Such a spear combines the advantage of the light shaft and a steel point that will retain its sharpness even after repeated throws. But be aware that repeated throws will eventually loosen the connection where the metal and the wood are joined.

MAKING MY OWN SPEAR

The three sticks I use for stick fighting are the 31-inch *yantok*, the 36-inch *yantok*, and the 44-inch *pingga*, so I chose to make spears with shafts of these lengths (Figure 70). For the tips, I used discarded blades from the Philippine balisong. (Since I practice with the balisong, I usually have a few with broken handles, and so I have blades that can be readily made into spearpoints.)

The balisong's blade is connected to the spear handle with two pins (Figure 71). A third pin is used as a stop to keep the balisong rigid when opened. I had to grind this third pin until it was flush with the blade, and then using a nail, I hammered it out from its hole.

I used a saw to cut away a slit (about 2 inches deep) on the wooden shaft, then widened the slit with a knife to accommodate the thickness of the blade. I placed the blade on the side of the shaft, marked the holes, then drilled them.

I inserted the blade in the slit, inserted a nail through each hole, and cut the excess lengths of the nails with a hacksaw. To prevent the nails from dropping out, I wrapped duct tape around them. However, since each nail is slightly smaller than the diameter of the hole in the blade, there is some movement in the connection. But it is tolerable.

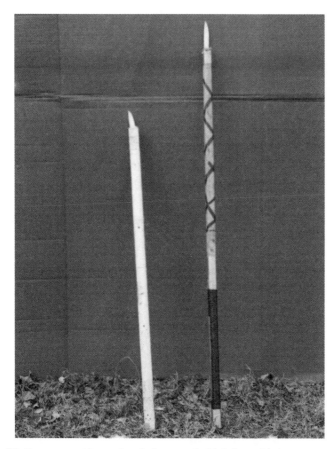

FIGURE 69. Two spears with wooden shafts topped with balisong blades.

Eventually, the nails will bend, then shear. When that happens, I can simply unwrap the duct tape and replace the nails.

The 44-inch spears I made cost me practically nothing since the wooden shafts I used were from pallets that were going to be thrown away. I made my 36-inch spears from

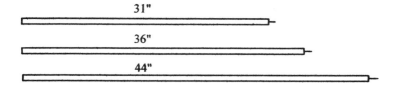

31"

36"

44"

FIGURE 70. The three lengths of spear I throw: overhand (top and middle) and underhand (bottom). My targets consist of eight layers (about 1 1/2" thick) of cardboard.

1" x 2" x 6' pine, which costs under $3. Alternatively, you can use the much heavier 1" x 2" x 4' red oak, which costs under $4, or the much lighter 1" x 2" x 4' poplar, which costs under $3. A box of sixty 6D finish nails cost about $1. A 60-yard roll of duct tape costs under $5.

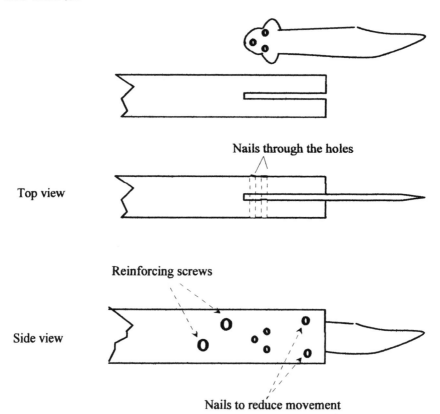

Nails through the holes

Top view

Reinforcing screws

Side view

Nails to reduce movement

FIGURE 71. Details of my spear head. I reinforced the wood with two screws to prevent it from splitting. However, I found later that there was no need for this. To reduce blade movement, I inserted the blade with only 2¹/₄" of its length showing and drilled a hole on each side, then inserted a nail in each hole. It is easier to make this kind of spear using wood with a rectangular cross section. The wood can be cut to the preferred length, trimmed, and the edges rounded to fit your grip.

GRIPPING A SPEAR

The grip on a spear will depend on the cross section of its shaft and on whether it is thrown overhand or underhand.

Grip in the overhand throw. The spear can be gripped at its CG and with its shaft resting on the thumb (Figure 72A). This will tilt the shaft downward. As a result, the spear has to be thrown at a steeper angle. This grip is better used on spears with small cross sections.

 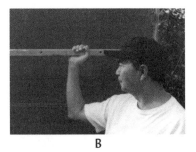

A   B

FIGURE 72. Grips on a spear in the overhand throw. In A, the spear rests on the thumb. I prefer to wrap my fingers around its shaft (B).

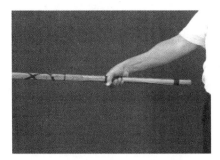

FIGURE 73. The grip I use on a spear in the underhand throw.

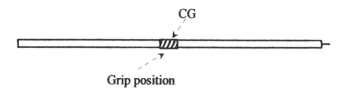

CG

Grip position

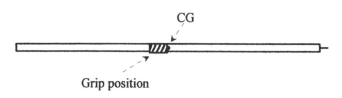

CG

Grip position

FIGURE 74. Grip positions in the overhand throw. A spear can be gripped at its CG (A). However, I prefer to throw a spear with the bottom of my fist touching its CG (B).

Spears with larger cross sections have to be gripped with the fingers wrapped around its shaft (Figure 72B). This will allow throwing the spear at a shallower angle. I grip the shaft with the bottom of my fist at its CG.

Grip in the underhand throw. I grip a 44-inch spear about three inches behind its CG (Figure 75A) when I throw it underhand from 17–26 feet. (This is analogous to gripping a knife with its heavier end, either the blade or the handle, to the front.) Also try gripping the spear farther back to hit the target point first from a farther distance (Figure 75B).

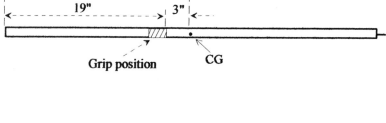

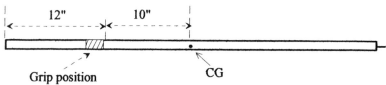

FIGURE 75. Grip positions in the underhand throw. I hold a 44-inch spear 19 inches from its lower end when I throw it from 17–26 feet (A); from farther away, 12 inches from its lower end (B).

THROWING A SPEAR

A throwing knife may be held so that at the time of release either its butt or its tip points in the direction of the target. On the other hand, if a spear is to hit point first, its tip must point toward the target at all times.

This means that the flight of the spear must be controlled such that it will have little or no rotation about its transverse and medial axes. However, to stabilize the spear in its flight, it has to be made to rotate around its longitudinal axis (Figure 76). This is achieved by making the spear roll inside the palm as the throw progresses.

The spear must be thrown in such a manner so as to prevent it from stalling or spinning. If the angle of attack (Figure 77A) is too steep or if it is held at the wrong location (Figure 77B), the tip of the spear will tend to rise causing it to stall.

Underhand throw. Throw a spear underhand such that at the time of release (a) its shaft is aligned with the ground, (b) its shaft does not come in contact with your forearm, and (c) your fingers are pointing at the target. Like the throwing of a knife, there is the required smooth follow-through.

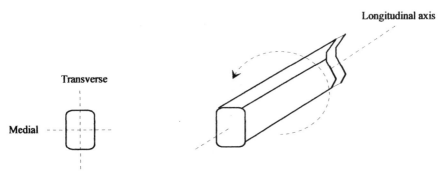

FIGURE 76. Axes of rotation of a spear. To stabilize a spear in flight in the underhand throw, it must be made to rotate about its longitudinal axis. In the overhand throw, this rotation is not necessary.

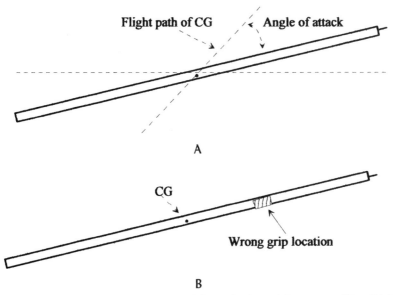

FIGURE 77. The tip of a spear will tend to rise if the angle of attack is too steep (A) or if it is gripped in the wrong location (B).

Wrist action (Figure 78) in the underhand throw is very important. In the beginning of the throw, the wrist must be relaxed. As the throw progresses, it bends more. At the time of release, the wrist is bent to the maximum—close to becoming uncomfortable.

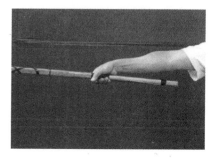

FIGURE 78. In the underhand throw, the wrist must be bent such that the spear leaves the hand parallel to the ground.

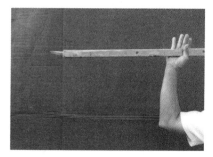

FIGURE 79. Grip change on the shaft in the overhand throw. The initial closed grip (Figure 72B) changes to the open grip at the time of release.

Overhand throw. In the overhand throw, at the time of release (a) a spear's shaft must be angled above the horizontal, (b) the fingers must be pointing at the target and (c) the spear must be perpendicular to the face of the target. At the time of release any slight motion to the right or left will cause the spear to drift to the side. In the required smooth follow-through, the open palm ends between the level of the shoulder and the hip.

Grip the spear, initially, with your fingers wrapped around its shaft and with the bottom of your fist at its CG. As the forward swing of your arm progresses, straighten your fingers (Figure 79) to allow the smooth release of the spear. To increase the power in the throw, lean your body forward but not to the point of imbalance.

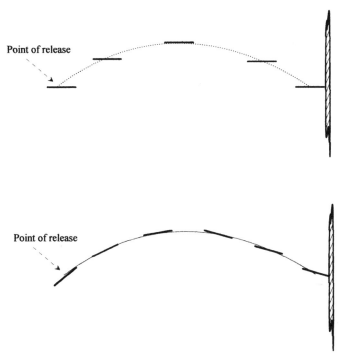

Point of release

Point of release

FIGURE 80. At close distances, a spear can be thrown so that it leaves the hand parallel to the ground (top). From farther away, it has to be released at a steeper angle (bottom). Otherwise, it will dip too fast.

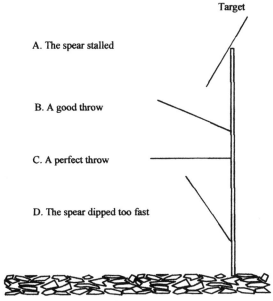

Target

A. The spear stalled

B. A good throw

C. A perfect throw

D. The spear dipped too fast

FIGURE 81. Possible angles of impact of a thrown spear.

Learning curve case study

I wanted to compare my underhand and overhand throws, so I generated this learning curve.

From the defensive standpoint (if you happen to have a spear at hand when there is a need for it), it is better to throw a spear underhand for the following reasons:

1. The underhand throw omits the act of raising the spear, which will save precious time.

2. The underhand throw is more likely to come as a surprise because the spear is held at the lower side and seems to pose no threat. On the other hand, the initial position of the spear in the overhand throw is very aggressive and threatening.

3. The spear is normally heavy.

Underhand vs. overhand throw. In the first month, my sticking percentage for the overhand throw was lower than for the underhand throw. However, in the subsequent months, I hardly missed sticking the spear in the overhand throw.

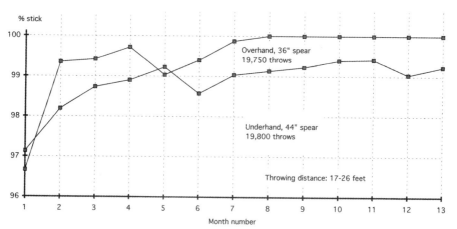

FIGURE 82. My sticking percentage for the right-hand overhand and underhand spear throws.

Underhand throw. The mechanics of the underhand throw are the same for any throwing implement. The timing of the release, the swing of the arm, and the smooth follow-through were merely carried over to my spear throws. Hence, the curve shows no frustration zone. (I learned to throw the bagakay, knife, ax, and spear in that order, so the frustration zone for my bagakay throws can be considered also as the frustration zone for my ax and spear throws.)

The spear is the easiest implement to stick on the target because it is easier to suppress its rotation (about its medial and transverse axes). Besides, the spear is initially held then thrown with its tip pointed at the target. On the other hand, the knife and the ax spin end over end on the way to the target making throwing distance critical. In the

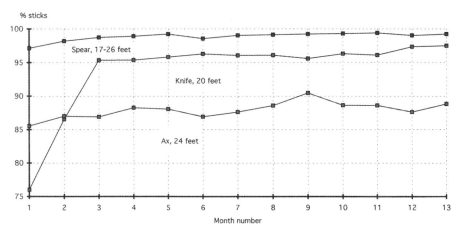

% sticks

FIGURE 83. A comparison of my sticking percentages for the right-hand underhand throws for the spear, ax, and knife.

spear throw, as long as you are able to get the spear to the target, there is a good chance that you can make it stick.

The knife has a more complex rotation than the ax. However, I have a better sticking average throwing the knife underhand. While the pendulum-like motion in the ax throw is the same as that in the spear throw, it is not easy to control the wobble of the ax because of its shape. Hence, I have a better sticking average with the knife.

The grips I used on the knife, ax, and spear are variations of the curled finger handle grips. In the ax and spear throws, my grip is behind the CG. On the knife, I place my thumb directly over its CG.

The throwing distance for the spear is *any* distance from which you can get the spear to the target. With the ax and the knife, it cannot be any distance: it must be such that it will allow both to make full spins.

3

Japanese Throwing Implements

While reading on the throwing of the Japanese shaken and shuriken, I came to recognize a major difference between the grips they use and the grips I use: the shuriken is gripped at the center of gravity.

I have thrown shuriken-like implements (such as the bagakay, ice picks, and chopsticks) before. However, I have gripped the throwing implement with its center of gravity just beyond my index finger's tip or about an inch away from it—not in my grasp. I decided to experiment with the Japanese method of gripping the shuriken.

The shuriken can be thrown in three ways: with no, half, or full spins. The no spin throw is particularly effective from as far as 18 feet. However, from longer distances, it becomes very difficult to get the shuriken to hit the target point first using this technique.

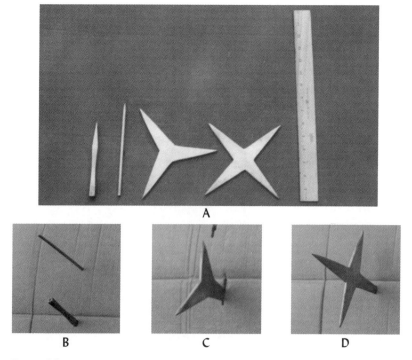

FIGURE 84. Japanese throwing implements (A) left to right: negishi-ryu shuriken, shirai-ryu shuriken, three-pointed shaken, and four-pointed shaken. Shown embedded on my cardboard targets are shirai-ryu and negishi-ryu shurikens (B), a three-pointed shaken (C), and a four-pointed shaken (D).

The one-pointed shuriken, when held with its point forward, will stick when it makes full spins; with its point toward the back, when it makes half spins. However, held one way or the other, the shuriken has to be thrown from a set distance.

The problem of distance is somewhat reduced when throwing a two-pointed shuriken, which obviously will stick whether it reaches the target on half or full spins. However, it still has to be thrown from a specific distance. This problem is magnified when the target is an enemy in motion.

An obvious solution to the problem of distance is the use of a many-pointed implement such as the shaken. The shaken will stick whether it makes full spins or fractions of a spin—from *any* distance.

Shuriken

The Japanese shuriken has its counterpart in the Philippine bagakay and Chinese flying sticker. The shuriken can be one- or two-pointed with lengths ranging from five to ten inches.

The shuriken can be flat, round, octagonal or with nonuniform cross sections. The shape of the shuriken identifies the particular Japanese martial arts school (Figure 84) that uses it.

The shuriken is relatively light; two or three can be carried without causing any discomfort. This will allow subsequent throws if the first throw misses or if faced by more than one opponent.

MAKING MY OWN SHURIKEN

The negishi-ryu shuriken and the shirai-ryu shuriken are not difficult to make.

Negishi-ryu shuriken. The negishi-ryu shuriken is not readily available in the United States. Fortunately, photographs and diagrams of negishi-ryu shurikens are illustrated in the book *Shuriken-Do* by the Japanese master Shirakami Ikku-ken.

I made wooden models of the negishi-ryu shurikens based on (a) the relative dimensions of the tapers and the flares, and (b) the length of the point that protrudes past the middle finger. Hence, built into the models are the lengths of my thumb and middle finger. After numerous filings and subsequent fittings, I felt confident that I could make a shuriken without ruining the first steel bar I would work on.

The negishi-ryu shuriken is held over the middle finger. It is squeezed by the index and ring fingers and pressed down with the thumb held nearly at right angles to the shuriken. I placed the bent thumb on the narrow waist. The negishi-ryu type shurikens I made are $5^5/8$ inches, 6 inches, and 8 inches long. Its point juts $3/4$-inch past the tip of my middle finger.

I made negishi-ryu type shurikens (Figure 85) from square steel bars. I had the steel bars cut to the proper length, rough-shaped the bars into shurikens with hexagonal cross sections using a file and a bench grinder, then smoothed them using a file and a belt sander.

Shirai-ryu shuriken. The shurikens of the shirai-ryu school have circular cross sections and are easier to make. Steel rods with lengths of thirty-six inches and with different diameters are readily available in hardware stores or in welding shops. A $1/4$-inch diameter 36-inch steel rod, in a hardware store, costs about \$4. In a welding shop, it costs less than half that. Even better is that the welding shop will cut the rod to the length you specify.

I tapered one end to a sharp point using a bench grinder (Figure 85).

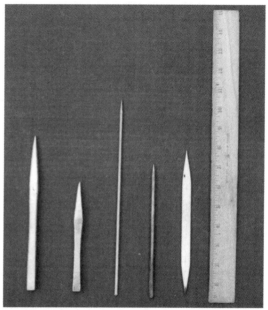

FIGURE 85. Typical shapes of a shuriken: negishi-ryu (left two), shirai-ryu (middle two), and Shirakami Ikku-ken's (right).

GRIPPING A SHURIKEN

A shuriken can be gripped with its sharp point up. It is held with a slight slant to the right with its length on the middle finger and is squeezed on each side by the index and ring fingers. At the same time, the thumb is placed on top to secure the grip.

It can also be gripped with its point on the palm. This kind of grip will not present any problem if you throw only occasionally. However, if you throw shurikens, say, one hundred times in one practice session, the repeated contact of the point on the palm can be annoying.

The shuriken can also be gripped like a knife or two-pointed bagakay. In these grips, either the dull end rests on the palm but not at its center or the sharp point is in the palm but its tip hardly touches the skin.

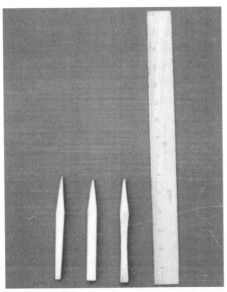

FIGURE 86. The shape of a shuriken will determine the speed of its release.

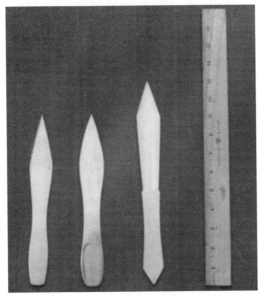

FIGURE 87. Swiss, German, and Spanish throwing knives with characteristic narrow waists.

The two grips on the shuriken (that are consistent with those I use on throwing knives) are:

1. Handle grip where the shuriken is held with its point away from the thrower

2. Blade grip where the shuriken is held with its point toward the thrower

The characteristics of the handle (Figure 86) will determine the speed of the release. For example, a shuriken with a tapered handle (Figure 86, left) should release quickly. If the grip is not tight enough, the thrown shuriken will fall short of the target. To avoid premature release, it should be gripped more tightly. A higher arc will compensate for a quick release. However, a higher arc could result in inaccurate throws.

If the shuriken tapers then flares (Figure 86, right), this will allow it to stay longer in the hand, thus allowing better control of the release. While the difference in release times is mere split seconds, this is the difference between a good and a bad throw.

The narrow waist of the shuriken ensures a consistent placement of the thumb from one throw to the next. Both the thumb and middle finger are placed on flared portions of the waist and of the point. If there is no flare, the thrower will need to squeeze harder on the shuriken to avoid a premature release.

A narrow waist is not unique to the shuriken but is also common in Swiss, German, and Spanish throwing knives (Figure 87). You can find this characteristic narrow waist on many American throwing knives as well.

Japanese masters' grips. There is a great difference between the grips used by American knife throwers (myself included) and those used by the Japanese master Shirakami Ikku-ken, shirai-ryu, and negishi-ryu. This will seem to be superficial. But it is not. It is more basic than that.

In these grips, the shuriken is held such that its CG is in the palm. American knife throwers grip the knife with the heavier end to the front. This places the CG of the knife at, close to, or an inch or two past the index finger.

Ikku-ken places the shuriken on top of his middle finger. This grip is very comfortable for shurikens with cross sections that approximate the size of the middle finger

A. NEGISHI-RYU GRIP.	B. JIKISHIN GRIP.	C. SHIRAI-RYU GRIP.
The dull end of the shuriken is placed at the center of the palm with the thumb pressing on its top and almost perpendicular to it.	The dull end is in the palm with the index finger held along its length. This is almost like pointing a finger and a very natural grip.	The sharp tip of the shuriken is in the palm.

FIGURE 88. Grips on the shuriken used by Japanese masters.

(Figure 88A). The shirai-ryu school uses this grip on a shuriken that has a small cross section (Figure 88C). One of the grips (Figure 88B) used by Shirakami Ikku-ken is quite unique. It is like pointing a finger at the target.

My grips. The general rule of thumb on gripping a knife or any throwing implement is to have the heavier end to the front (Figure 89).

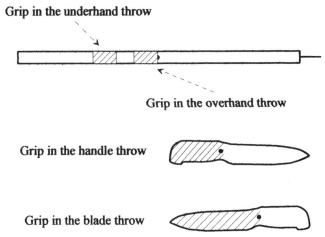

Grip in the underhand throw

Grip in the overhand throw

Grip in the handle throw

Grip in the blade throw

FIGURE 89. The rule of thumb in throwing an implement is to have the heavier end to the front. The crosshatch is the hand grip on the implement.

I follow this rule when I throw a 7-inch shuriken (Figure 90A–B). This shuriken is light and the only way I feel comfortable throwing it is to hold it such that its dull tip rests on the edge of my ring finger (close to the little finger). Thus, its CG is about half an inch past the tip of my thumb. This gives me the feeling that I am throwing something.

The handle grips I use on a shuriken (Figure 91B, D) with the CG at, close to, or an inch or two past the tip of my thumb or index finger will make it an effective weapon in close-quarter fighting.

A   B

FIGURE 90. I throw a 7" shirai-ryu shuriken with its CG about half an inch past the tip of my thumb.

THROWING A SHURIKEN

A light 6-inch shuriken should be thrown overhand. A longer and heavier shuriken can be thrown underhand without any problem.

The shuriken will spin counterclockwise (viewed from the right side of the thrower) about its CG when thrown overhand. This spin is imparted to the shuriken by the rotation of the throwing arm about the shoulder.

A shuriken may be thrown with no spin, half spins, or full spins.

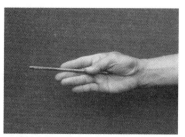

A. This is similar to the straight finger blade grip I use on the bagakay. However, Japanese masters keep their thumbs almost perpendicular to the shuriken. My thumb is more on a diagonal.

B. The dull end is in the palm with the thumb held on top of the shuriken. This is the curled finger handle grip that I also use on the knife. This same grip can be used for close-quarter fighting. (See Figure 90A.)

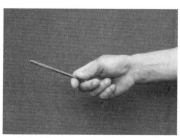

C. The sharp tip is in the palm but barely touches it. This is the same curled finger blade grip I use on the knife. (See Figure 90B.)

D. The dull end of the 8" negishi-ryu shuriken is in the palm. This is the curled finger handle grip I also use on the knife.

FIGURE 91. The grips I use on the shuriken.

No spin. In the no spin throw, a shuriken is gripped with its point toward the target in much the same way as when a spear is thrown. For the no spin throw, horsehair is attached to the tail of the shuriken. Even with such artifice, the thrower still has to apply moderate pressure with the index finger on the tail at the time of release to suppress its spin.

I throw the negishi-ryu shuriken at an angle of launch such that it will stall and just start to dip close to the target. This is accomplished by an abrupt downward movement of the throwing arm at the time of release. The index finger will prevent the shuriken from rotating. *This no spin throw can only be effected if the shuriken is released with the hand on a vertical.*

The no spin adds two more variables to a throw: the horsehair and the need to suppress the shuriken's spin; therefore it is more difficult than either the half or full spin throw.

To be considered as a no spin throw, the implement has to be thrown from a minimum distance of 17 feet.

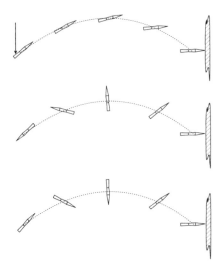

FIGURE 92. The trajectory of a one-pointed shuriken making no spin (top), half spin (middle), and one full spin (bottom). The downward arrow (top) indicates pressure applied with the index finger on the shuriken to suppress its spin.

Half spin. In the half spin throw, the shuriken is gripped with its point toward the thrower (in much the same way that a knife is thrown by the blade). This is an easier throw than the no spin throw.

Full spin. In the full spin throw, the shuriken is gripped with its point toward the target (in much the same way that a knife is thrown by the handle). This is the more practical throw for the shuriken, if it is to double as a weapon for close-quarter fighting. In books on the shuriken written by Japanese authors, its use in close-quarter fighting has been mentioned.

The shuriken is easier to throw if you allow it to spin end over end. However, like the throwing of any implement (except for the shaken or the spear), to make it stick, it has to be thrown from a given distance.

THROWING DISTANCE

I do not have firsthand contact with the negishi-ryu school. However, Shirakami Ikku-ken has summarized the negishi-ryu shuriken and their throwing methods. Essentially,

1. The negishi-ryu throws the shuriken using the "direct" hit method. Direct hit means no spin. The maximum throwing distance according to the Japanese master is 18.1 feet.

2. The negishi-ryu uses shurikens that have tassels made from threads and from bear or horsehair, which according to their lengths are made for throwing from a short, middle, or long distances. The length of the tassel determines the location of the

center of gravity of the shuriken. The school uses shurikens with no tails for throwing from a short distance.

3. The negishi-ryu trains to throw from a long distance a shuriken designed for throwing from a short distance.

The throwing distance will depend on (a) the grip used on the implement, (b) the location of its CG, and to a lesser extent (c) length of the implement. The effect of the grip used on the throwing (sticking) distance is illustrated in Table 7.

TABLE 7. GRIPS AND THROWING DISTANCES USING
ONE- AND TWO-POINTED 8" NEGISHI-RYU TYPE SHURIKEN.

Number of spins	Grip		Distance*, feet
	one-pointed	two-pointed	
0	handle	handle or blade	
$1/2$	blade	handle or blade	9
1	handle	handle or blade	21
$1^1/2$	blade	handle or blade	28
2	handle	handle or blade	40

* See Chapter 1, "Throwing and sticking distances."

What grip would you use to throw from 15', 25', 35', and other "in-between" distances?

The in-between distances can be bridged with a shift of the location of the CG, not within the shuriken (effected by varying the length of the tassel) but by gripping it farther up or down the handle. Therefore a longer negishi-ryu shuriken makes more sense, otherwise, you could run out of shuriken to hold. For this reason, I used an 8-inch shuriken to generate Table 7.

It is obvious that it is more efficient to throw a two-pointed shuriken than one with only one point, since you do not need to switch from the handle to the blade grip. Or better yet, throw the many-pointed shaken instead.

LEARNING CURVE CASE STUDY

No spin vs. with spin throw. From Figure 96, it is apparent that the no spin throw becomes less accurate when the distance is greater than 18 feet. Hence, at longer distances, the half spin or full spin throws are more practical.

In Figure 97, I compared my sticking percentage for the no spin and the two full spins throw. However, I used a longer shuriken in the full spins throw and a shorter shuriken in the no spin throw.

Throwing an 8-inch shuriken from 22 feet with no spin, I tried hard to suppress its spin, but I couldn't. This is understandable, because the CG of the longer shuriken is more to the front than that of the shorter shuriken. I also tried throwing a 5⅝-inch shuriken, with two full spins, from 21 feet. However, the 8-inch shuriken is more accurate from longer distances than the shorter shuriken.

Shirakami Ikku-ken does not mention throwing the negishi-ryu shuriken other than in the no spin throw. However, I found that the 8-inch and the 5⅝-inch shurikens work well with the underhand throw.

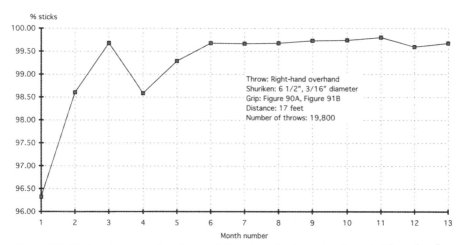

FIGURE 93. My learning curve throwing a shirai-ryu type shuriken using the curled finger handle grip (Figures 90A, 91B).

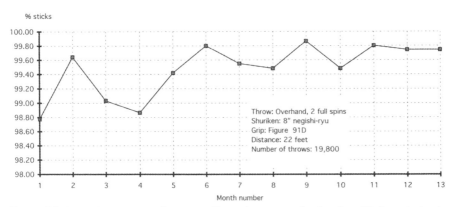

FIGURE 94. My sticking average throwing a 8" negishi-ryu type shuriken from 22 feet gripping it in the same way as when I throw a knife by the handle.

Figure 97 shows my averages for the no spin and the two full spins throw. The graph indicates that at longer distances, it is more practical, indeed necessary, to throw a shuriken with a spin.

LEARNING CURVE CASE STUDY

Jikishin grip. The jikishin grip (Figure 88B) is the name used by Shirakami Ikku-ken for when the shuriken is held with its dull end on the palm and with the index finger placed along its length. Ikku-ken does not mention the distance from which he used this grip. Nor does he mention if he threw it with a spin.

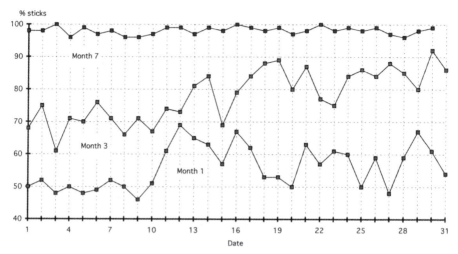

FIGURE 95. My sticking percentage for three nonconsecutive months throwing a 5⅝" negishi-ryu type shuriken with no spin from 18 feet using the negishi-ryu grip (Figure 88A).

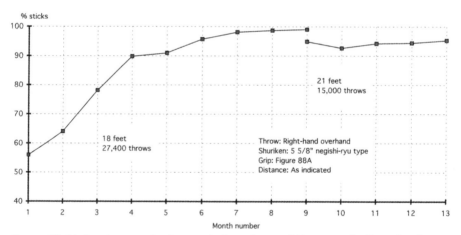

FIGURE 96. My learning curve for the no spin throw for a negishi-ryu type shuriken using the negishi-ryu grip. There is a big difference in my averages throwing the 5⅝" shuriken from 18 feet and from 21 feet.

I thought that, since its CG is on my palm, I would be able to throw the shuriken with no spin in much the same way when I used the negishi-ryu grip. However, I was not able to suppress its spin.

After several throws, I determined that the first throwing distance, using this grip on a 5⅝-inch negishi-ryu shuriken is about 24 feet. From this distance, it takes a full spin before it will stick on the target. The next throwing distance is about 52 feet, which is not practical for a defensive throw—unless you are throwing from ambush.

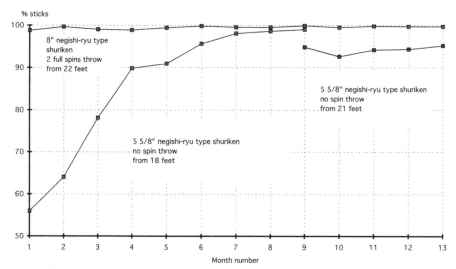

FIGURE 97. A comparison of my sticking averages throwing a 5⁵/₈" shuriken using the no spin throw and the full spins throw.

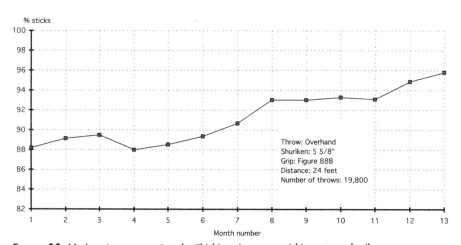

FIGURE 98. My learning curve using the jikishin grip on a negishi-ryu type shuriken.

Note that in the jikishin grip, the shuriken starts to spin after it has passed the midpoint of the throw.

Shaken

A knife thrown in the blade grip will stick on a target if it completes ¹/₂, 1¹/₂, 2¹/₂ spins and so on. A knife (or ax) thrown in the handle grip will stick when it completes 1, 2, 3 spins and so on. See Figure 17. This means that for a knife to stick on the target, it must be thrown from a certain distance.

Spinning is not the desired behavior if a spear is to stick to the target. It has to be held and thrown with its tip pointing in the direction of the target at all times.

Unlike a knife or an ax, a bagakay, because it is two-pointed, will stick on the target when it completes $1/2$, 1, $1^1/2$, 2, $2^1/2$, 3, . . . spins. It is obvious then that (if the distance to the target is not known) there is a greater possibility of a two-pointed throwing implement sticking on a target than a one-pointed one.

It follows that if a throwing implement is many-pointed, it will be easier to make it stick on the target. The implement will stick after any number of full spins or fractions of spins. It does not matter what the distance is from where it is thrown. Such an implement will be an ideal defensive throwing weapon because distances are never constant in a conflict. Two such throwing implements are the Chinese throwing star and the Japanese shaken.

A shaken can have three, four, five, six, or as many as eight projecting points (Figure 99). One will rarely miss sticking it. The only disadvantage of the shaken is that it is not convenient to carry. If accessed improperly, the carrier could get pricked or even stabbed by its many sharp points.

Shakens sold commercially are usually small and lighter than a throwing knife. However, what they lack in mass, they make up for in the number that can be carried on one's person and the rapid succession with which they can be thrown.

Making my own shakens

I fabricate my own shakens because the shakens available in the market only partially satisfy the characteristics that I am looking for. I make my shakens with dull edges that allow more gripping options. For example, you cannot use the grips shown in Figures 103 and 106 on shakens with sharp edges.

I started with $3/16$-inch thick rectangular steel plates that measured 12" x $6^1/2$", which were cut for me by the welding shop where I bought them. I made wooden models of the shakens. After I fitted and felt comfortable with the wooden model, I traced it on the steel plate.

Shakens can have holes in the middle through which a cord can be run for ease of carrying. A piece of wood can be inserted in the hole to make it easier to pull out deeply embedded shakens. The hole also allows a more secure grip.

While throwing regular-size shakens, I wondered how it would feel to throw bigger ones, so I made a few that are oversized. The $8^1/8$-inch four-pointed shakens I made dwarf those that are sold in martial arts stores. Because the oversized shaken is big, it is also heavy. Thus, it can be thrown underhand and will stick with authority. It packs quite a wallop.

Gripping a shaken

A shaken can be gripped in a number of ways for throwing (Figures 100–103): The grips illustrated will give you good control over the shaken. Your choice of grip will depend on the size of the shaken, the number of projecting points, and whether it has dull or sharp edges.

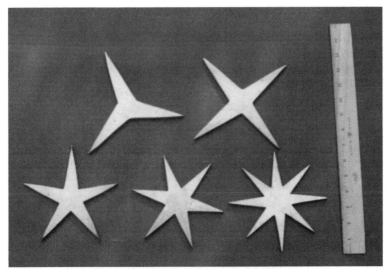

FIGURE 99. Many-pointed shakens are easy enough to make. Since I used a hacksaw, I cut the steel at the rate of 7" a day. The maximum depth of penetration decreases as the number of projecting points increases because adjacent projecting points on each side of the one that sticks could get in the way (Figure 104, bottom).

In the overhand throw, a shaken is supported on the "V" of the hand with the index finger and thumb touching (Figure 103A–D). The middle three fingers are placed on top of one projecting point. The little finger barely touches the shaken at the back. This allows a more secure grip for use of the shaken in close-quarter fighting and better control for throwing.

In the underhand throw, the shaken rests on the index, middle, and ring fingers (Figure 103E).

THROWING A SHAKEN

A shaken can be thrown overhand or underhand from the left or from the right using the grip of your choice. Since a shaken will stick from whatever distance it is thrown, the thrower can concentrate on hitting a small area of the target and need not be concerned with whether it will stick or not.

The mechanics of a shaken throw are the same as those for a knife, ax, or spear. The feet must be spaced apart and the knees bent comfortably. For the shaken to stick with authority:

1. The knees must unbend slightly in the underhand throw and bend slightly in the overhand throw

2. The hips must twist to reinforce the subsequent elbow action

3. The release and follow-through must be smooth

4. Balance must be maintained at all times.

FIGURE 100. The most common grip used on small sharp-edged shakens. The thumb and index finger are placed on opposite sides of the hole.

FIGURE 101. The grip used by the Japanese master Shirakami Ikku-ken on oversized, dull-edged shakens. The last three fingers grip one of the projecting points. The thumb and index finger are held straight on opposite sides.

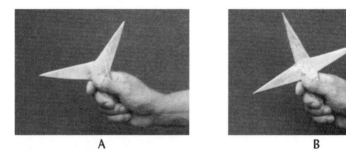

A   B

FIGURE 102. Knifelike grips on many-pointed, dull-edged, oversized shakens. The shaken is gripped at one of its projecting points with the four fingers and the thumb.

The throwing action must be such that at the time of release, the wrist is kept in one plane. Any inward or outward bending of the wrist will make the shaken wobble in its flight.

The shaken can be thrown horizontally, vertically, or diagonally.

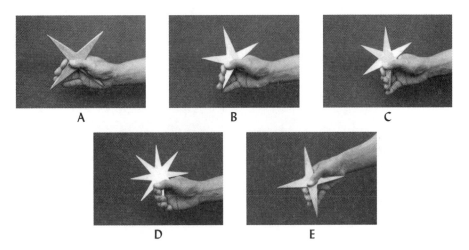

FIGURE 103. The overhand (A–D) and underhand (E) grips I use on oversized, dull-edged shakens.

The target must be small enough for you to develop accuracy in placing the shaken but still big enough to minimize the possibility of an incoming shaken hitting an already-embedded one. You can use the multiple targets shown in Figure 42. Sometimes I use rectangular 10" x 12" targets for the smaller three- and four-pointed shakens, and 12"x 14" targets for the bigger shakens. Mark the dimensions on the cardboard; then connect the dots. To further develop accuracy, use concentric rectangles.

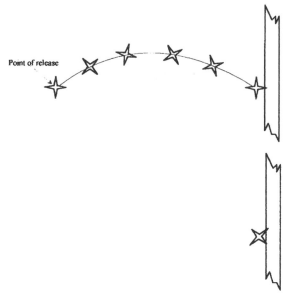

FIGURE 104. Trajectory of a shaken. The shaken will stick whether it hits the target in fractions of a spin or in full spins.

The shaken could hit with two of its points simultaneously sticking on the target (Figure 104, bottom). This requires replacing the cardboard target more often than when you throw one- or two-pointed implements.

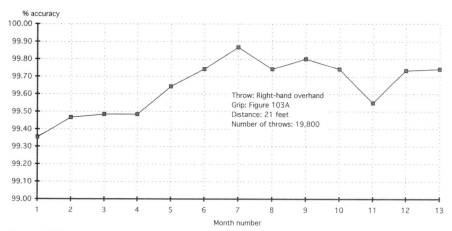

FIGURE 105. My accuracy percentage throwing a four-pointed (5" across) shaken. The target is a 10" x 12" rectangle.

Overhand throw using Ikku-ken's grip. The jikishin grip (Figure 88B) used by the Japanese master Ikku-ken on the one-pointed shuriken and the grip (Figure 101) he used on the four-pointed shaken are identical.

I was skeptical when I first saw the jikishin grip for the one-pointed shuriken. However, after having used the grip, I came to appreciate its merits. I thought it would be interesting to throw a three-pointed shaken using the same grip (Figure 106).

Then I came to appreciate its merits even more.

FIGURE 106. The grip I used on a three-pointed shaken.

You will be less accurate with the three-pointed shaken than with the four-pointed shaken for two reasons. First, the same-size three-pointed shaken is at least 25 percent lighter than a four-pointed shaken. Second, the three-pointed shaken could hit "flat" as shown in Figure 107.

The lighter three-pointed shaken will pop out (more often than the four-pointed shaken) of the cardboard target even after hitting with its point.

FIGURE 107. The adjacent projecting points of a three-pointed shaken are farther apart than those of a four-pointed shaken.

Commercial 4-inch shaken thrown from beside the left hip. Shakens sold commercially have needle-sharp points and razor-sharp edges. When you practice throwing them, you must exercise caution.

The most common way of throwing sharp-edged shakens is from beside the left hip. I have thrown knives the same way. However, knives are easier to throw because they are much heavier.

Because shakens are light, they must be thrown energetically. The power in the throw is derived from the twisting of the hips, the straightening of the arm, and the unbending of the wrist.

If you have not thrown a shaken from this position before, expect to hurt the next day. The pain in the upper arm, sometimes in the shoulder joint, is tolerable but annoying. However, after a couple of days, it will go away.

In my first fifty throws, the shakens drifted to my right. To compensate for the drift, I moved about a foot to my left. In this throwing position my front toe was pointed toward the target. However, I prefer to throw the shaken with my right side at a right angle with the target. This throwing position minimizes the drift to the right.

4

Chinese Throwing Implements

The Chinese martial arts are well-known for empty hand fighting systems as well as for weapons fighting systems. A wide variety of weapons, including swords, spears, knives, and staffs of varying sizes and shapes are part of the Chinese weapons fighting tradition.

While many Chinese weapons and empty hand fighting systems have become household words, there is a little known branch of study called hidden weapons. These weapons are "hidden" in the sense that they are carried covertly on one's person and become visible only at the time of use or they are visible but are not designed for use as weapons or are so commonplace that most people will not consider them weapons (ordinary pebbles, for example).

This branch includes an extensive array of weapons, which can be grouped under three categories:

1. Weapons used to launch projectiles. These include the cylindrical dart, slingshot, bow and arrow, blowgun, and crossbow.

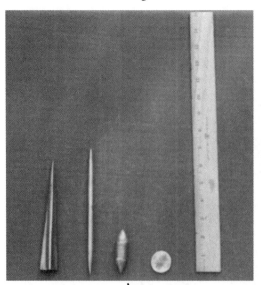

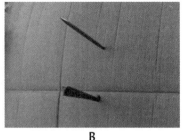

B

A

FIGURE 108. Chinese throwing implements: (A, left to right) flying dart, flying sticker, flying olive, and golden coin dart. With practice, the flying dart and flying sticker can be made to stick on cardboard targets (B). However, it would take some sort of Herculean effort to get a golden coin dart or steel olive to stick on a cardboard target. The ideal target for the olive and the coin is a mound of earth or clay.

2. Weapons that are thrown but are tethered to a rope for quick recovery. These include the flying cymbal, mace, flying claw, rope dart, shooting star hammer, dragon's beard hook, whip-chain dart, and iron lotus.

3. Weapons that are thrown free of tethers from the hand. These include the flying dart, golden coin dart, flying steel olive, and flying sticker.

We will focus on the hidden weapons that are thrown freely. Of these hidden weapons, we will look at the flying dart, because of its unique shape and the unique method with which it has to be thrown; the steel olive and golden coin dart, because of their unique shape and size: and the flying sticker, because of the unique grip with which it is thrown.

Flying dart

The flying dart has a most unique shape. It has a "Y" cross section that tapers to a point. Two-inch long red and green silk tassels can be attached to a flying dart, which help suppress its natural tendency to spin.

The flying dart is usually less than 4 inches long and weighs about 6 ounces. Because it is relatively short and light, Chinese masters in the past carried a set of twelve or nine darts. In each set there is one flying dart that is longer and heavier than the rest that is used to deliver the *coup de grâce*.

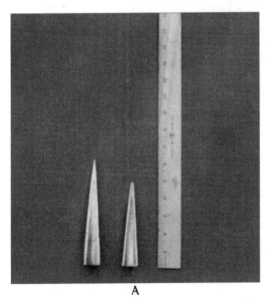
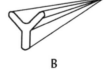

B

A

FIGURE 109. Flying darts I fabricated from solid steel bars (A). The three grooves (B) make the dart unique.

MAKING MY OWN FLYING DARTS

It is difficult to find flying darts in the United States. I have a feeling that even in China, they may be difficult to find. So, you will most likely need to make your own.

I first made a 5-inch long wooden model. The making of the wooden model helped me plan how to execute the minimum number of cuts since I planned to construct my dart from a solid steel bar. I hacksawed, filed, ground, and smoothed the 1" x 1" cross section steel bar until, finally, I was able to finish one flying dart after a month.

GRIPPING A FLYING DART

A flying dart can be gripped so that the middle finger is placed over the top groove and the thumb held perpendicular to the back fin (Figure 110). The ring and index fingers press on opposite sides of the dart at the top. This is similar to the grip used on a negishi-ryu shuriken where the shuriken is placed over the middle finger, squeezed with the index and ring fingers on each side, and pressed with the thumb on top (Figure 88A).

I prefer to grip a flying dart with my thumb pressing on the left groove (Figure 111).

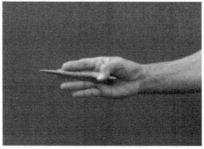

FIGURE 110. One of the grips that can be used on the flying dart where the thumb presses on one of the vanes.

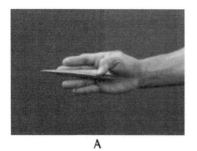
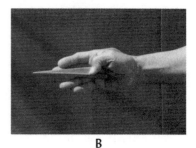

A   B

FIGURE 111. The grip I use on the flying dart. The middle finger is placed over the top groove. The dart is squeezed in place with the thumb on the left groove. The ring and index fingers (held straight) press at opposite sides at the top. The tail end is placed in the middle of the palm.

THROWING A FLYING DART

The traditional target for flying darts is 6 feet tall and 7 inches wide. Seven circles are drawn on the target. The biggest circle has a diameter of six inches and has a 1.5-inch red heart inside; the smallest has a diameter of one inch and has a 0.3-inch red heart.

The flying dart can be thrown in two ways: with the palm facing up (positive hand) or with the palm facing down (negative hand) with spin or without spin. The positive hand throw on a dart that weighs more than 6 ounces is unique to the Chinese martial arts.

With spin throw. The positive hand throw is not an easy throw and requires great wrist strength. Indeed, the development of wrist strength is part of the training for the positive hand throw. Chinese masters have developed their wrists such that they can throw flying darts accurately with the positive hand from as far as 40 feet.

The required wrist strength implies that the wrist bends at the time of release, which means that the dart will spin when thrown from 40 feet.

No spin throw. I tried throwing the flying dart with my palm facing up but I felt I did not have control over its release. I feel I have better control throwing it with the negative hand.

In my first throw, my dart stalled and hit sideways. On my ninetieth throw, I became aware of the dart's rotation along its longitudinal axis. I tried to duplicate it. Sometimes I was able to make the dart rotate along its longitudinal axis. At other times, it stalled. I was puzzled. After many throws, I found that when I pressed too hard on the left groove with my thumb, the dart stalled. When I decreased the pressure, the dart rotated along its longitudinal axis.

There is a simple explanation for this rotation. The clockwise (as viewed from the back of the thrower) rotation of a flying dart is imparted to it by the clockwise rotation of the throwing arm as it traces a circular arc. This rotation along its longitudinal axis is not necessary for the flying dart to stick, but it looks nice as it corkscrews toward the target.

The flying dart can only be thrown with no spin (a) from a close distance and (b) if the wrist is kept rigid at the time of release. Any bend in the wrist will cause the dart to spin.

LEARNING CURVE CASE STUDY

It is very difficult to throw a flying dart with no spin. Indeed, in my first 100 throws I was able to stick a flying dart only four times.

I threw the dart from 17 feet. Since the experience was new to me, at the same time that I was trying to make it stick, I was studying its behavior in flight.

I used one 5-inch and two 6-inch flying darts to generate Figure 112. The two lengths throw equally well from 17 feet.

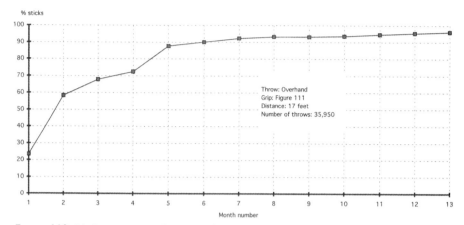

FIGURE 112. My learning curve throwing a flying dart using the negative hand. I used a set of concentric circles, the outermost of which was 8" in diameter. I omitted the heart and substituted a circle with a diameter of 3". Rather than draw the circles, I pasted photocopies of the concentric circles on my cardboard targets.

Golden coin dart

The golden coin dart as used in Chinese martial arts can be one of two kinds: a real coin used as money or a coin with sharp edges. They are both light. Even lighter are the coins with holes in the middle.

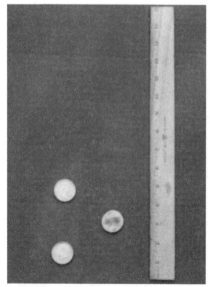

FIGURE 113. Coins that I throw. The 1 1/8" diameter, 1/16" thick John F. Kennedy and Benjamin Franklin half-dollars are at the left. At the right is a coin-sized thrower I use as a substitute for a Chinese golden coin dart.

A sharp coin dart can deliver quite a sting. On the other hand, a light, dull-edged real coin will have to be thrown vigorously if it is to have an effect on the outcome of a fight. The golden coin dart may be replaced with a heavier coinlike implement, which can be made thicker to increase its potency as a throwing weapon.

MAKING A GOLDEN COIN DART

I made ¹⁄₈" thick "coins" from steel plates. These coins are considerably thicker than the JFK half-dollar but of the same diameter. I made twenty coins because I expected to lose some since I throw on grass. To help locate them, I sprayed the coins with orange fluorescent paint.

I tapered the edge until it was nearly sharp. Sharp coins have to be carried in a special pouch as they can easily put holes in the pocket and, if accessed carelessly, can also easily cut fingers.

GRIPPING A GOLDEN COIN DART

A golden coin dart can be gripped between the thumb and index finger (Figure 114A). As many as three golden coin darts can be placed between the knuckles (Figure 114B) where the sharp edges just clear the inside of the palm.

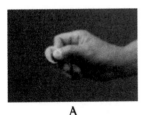  

| A | B | C |

FIGURE 114. Grips on a golden coin dart. Sharp-edged coins can be gripped between the thumb and the index finger (A) or between the knuckles (B). Coins with dull edges can be gripped in the manner shown in C, which is very much like the grip used on a baseball.

THROWING A GOLDEN COIN DART

Kungfu masters in the past favored throwing the golden coin dart with a positive hand. However, there is no reason why they cannot be thrown with a negative hand.

As many as four golden coin darts can be thrown simultaneously to ensure that the enemy is not able to avoid getting hit. It is for the same reason that the Philippine bagakays are thrown five at a time.

In throws using the grips in Figure 114A–B, coins will wobble toward the target and will seem to travel in slow motion. Nevertheless, these grips are good for close-quarter throws. From a greater distance, I prefer gripping dull-edged coins as in Figure 114C. With this grip, I am able to give a coin a vigorous rotation (which is needed) because it is very light.

You do not need to make your own golden coin darts. You can use the JFK half-dollar. However, make sure to coat the coin with bright paint. Otherwise, it will be difficult to find when you throw on grass.

LEARNING CURVE CASE STUDY

The ideal target for a golden coin dart is clay or a mound of earth, because on impact, the coin will become embedded on such a target. However, it is not easy to set up a clay target. If you use an 8" circle pasted on cardboard, note that the coins will simply bounce off.

Golden coin darts can be thrown one or more at a time. When several are thrown at a time, an adversary can be hit even if he takes evasive action.

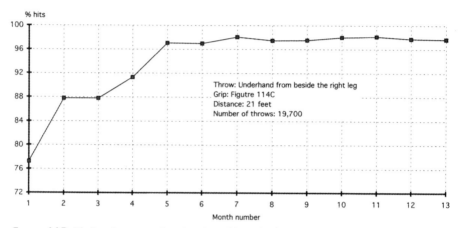

Throw: Underhand from beside the right leg
Grip: Figutre 114C
Distance: 21 feet
Number of throws: 19,700

FIGURE 115. My learning curve throwing the golden coin dart.

Flying steel olive

The steel olive was a very popular weapon among kungfu practitioners during the Ching and Ming Dynasties. Also known as the Chinese flying olive, they are shaped like a nut. Being pointed at both ends like a nail, they are also called nail-nuts. They are made of steel and are relatively heavy for their size of about $2^{1}/_{2}$-inches long and with a diameter of about 1 inch. Since they are small, they are easily concealed. Several are normally carried in a bag.

MAKING A STEEL OLIVE

I bought a $^{3}/_{4}$" diameter 24"-long steel rod from a welding shop and cut it into $2^{1}/_{4}$"-long sections. Since I do not have a lathe, I tapered the two ends into a point using a file; then smoothed it all using a belt sander.

I made two other types of throwing implements that approximated the size of the traditional steel olive using $^{1}/_{2}$" x $^{1}/_{2}$" and 1" x 1" solid steel bars. These are shown in Figure 116.

Coat your steel olives with fluorescent paint because they can be easily lost on grass. Recoat the olives every so often as needed, to keep them visible.

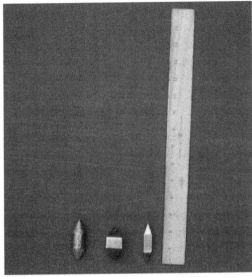

FIGURE 116. The steel olive I made is 2¹/₄ inches long and has a ³/₄ inch diameter (left). At middle and right are two other throwers I made with square cross sections.

GRIPPING A STEEL OLIVE

Kungfu practitioners hold the steel olive with the thumb, index finger, and middle finger (Figure 117). Try this grip; however, you may feel more comfortable with the grip shown in Figure 118 where I cradle the steel olive on my ring, middle, and index fingers and press it down with the thumb. The conical ends fit perfectly in my hand.

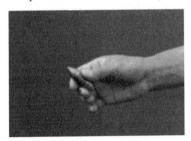

FIGURE 117. Three-finger grip on a steel olive.

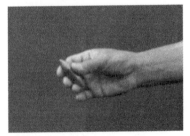

Figure 118. You may obtain better control on the release of a steel olive by gripping it with four fingers.

THROWING A STEEL OLIVE

The steel olive is short and stubby. As a defensive weapon, it is designed to disable by concussion. Though pointed at both ends, it cannot inflict the deep puncture wounds that a thin sharp knife or a flying sticker could. However, the 2¹/₂"-long ³/₄" diameter steel olive is heavy enough to deliver a knockout blow.

I use eight layers of cardboard with no spaces between them when I throw wedge-like throwing implements such as knives or even bagakays. But steel olives thrown at such a target will simply bounce off it. Instead insert a crumpled piece of paper between the second and third layers thus creating space between them. With this arrangement, when the olive hits point first (or even sideways), it will become embedded on the target. Still, even with this modified target, the steel olive will often pop out of the target.

The ideal target for steel olives is clay or a mound of earth. However, if you do not have this kind of target, you'll need to replace the first two layers of cardboard (which will become mutilated after every twenty throws) frequently.

The steel olive can be thrown in such a way as to give it a pronounced rotation about its longitudinal axis (like the spin of a football). Or it can be made to spin end over end.

The number of spins that a knife, ax, or shuriken make as it speeds toward the target can be counted visually by an observer or with the help of a movie camera. Not so for the steel olive.

The steel olive spins end over end very fast. Hence, even if it hits point first, it will pop out of a cardboard target. However, while the desired result in throwing the steel olive is to make it hit the target point first, you may choose to make your goal a more modest one: to hit the designated target without regard to the olive's orientation at impact.

Throwing a steel olive is similar to throwing a ball or a stone. The stone does not have to stick to the target; it must merely hit the designated spot. For example: if my target measures 8¹/₂" x 11", I count a throw as a hit if the steel olive makes an impact inside the lines.

LEARNING CURVE CASE STUDY

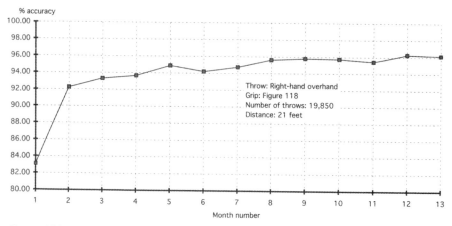

FIGURE 119. My learning curve for throwing a steel olive. The target is 8¹/₂" wide and 11" tall.

The steel olive will not stick on a cardboard target. Still, hitting the target will be a test of skill.

At one time, one of my students asked me, "If you are to carry a knife on your person, which one will it be?" My answer was, "I would rather bring the steel olive."

Flying sticker

The Chinese flying sticker was created during the Ching Dynasty and was a popular weapon among kungfu fighters. It was an adaptation of a sticker used for fighting in water.

A flying sticker is cigar-shaped and sharp at both ends. It is 7" long and has a ¹/₄" diameter. The 7-inch flying sticker is but a shorter version of the Philippine 10-inch bagakay. Being relatively light (about 6 ounces), twelve flying stickers are normally carried, hidden, on the shoulder or around the waist.

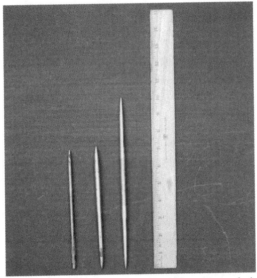

FIGURE 120. The flying sticker (middle) is cigar-shaped but thinner. At left is a throwing needle with its tassel removed. At right is a 10" bagakay.

MAKING A FLYING STICKER

Flying stickers are not commercially available so you will have to make your own.

Buy ¹/₄ inch diameter steel rods from a hardware store and cut them into 7 inch lengths. Taper both ends into 1¹/₂ inch tall cones using a bench grinder or a file. Smooth the cones using a belt sander or sandpaper. Do not make the points too sharp.

GRIPPING A FLYING STICKER

A sticker used for fighting in water has a ring at its middle. The middle finger is inserted in the ring to secure it; then the fingers are wrapped around its middle. This grip was carried over to the flying sticker.

FIGURE 121. A flying sticker is gripped in the middle with all fingers wrapped around it. About 1 1/2 inches of its length protrudes past the bottom and top of the fist.

A flying sticker has no ring since it was designed to be thrown. Still, it is held in the middle also (Figure 121).

What makes throwing a flying sticker unique is the location of the grip.

THROWING A FLYING STICKER

A flying sticker will stick on the target when it makes full spins. My first throwing distance for the two-pointed flying sticker is about 12 feet. From this distance, the sticker will complete one full spin and hit the target with its point (held initially toward the front). The second, third, or fourth throwing distance can be calculated using Equation 1, which was discussed in Chapter 1.

A flying sticker, because it is two-pointed, will also stick on the target when it makes half spins. My first throwing distance for the two-pointed flying sticker in the half spin throw is 8 feet. From this distance, the point of the sticker (the one initially held toward the thrower) will stick on the target. With an arm reach of 2 feet, my sticking distance is 6 feet.

The next (second farther) distance to throw it from to make it stick is 20 feet. This can be calculated from Equation 3 (page 26) using the given values of n (1), Z (6), and arm reach (2). From 20 feet, the sticker will make 1 1/2 spins, and its point will hit the target.

LEARNING CURVE CASE STUDY

In the beginning, I was not comfortable throwing the flying sticker, and it showed in my sticking average. Sometimes, I would look at the embedded stickers and find that four hit the target after making 1 1/2 spins. However, the fifth hit the target after making two full spins.

I had thought that I was throwing the sticker with consistency, so to find four hitting with 1 1/2 spins and a fifth hitting with two full spins was exasperating. However, after 2,000 throws, I was able to consistently hit the target with flying stickers making 1 1/2 spins only. At that time, I began to appreciate the merits of the grip.

It is apparent that this grip in the middle is very sensitive to small changes in sticking distance and in the location of the grip.

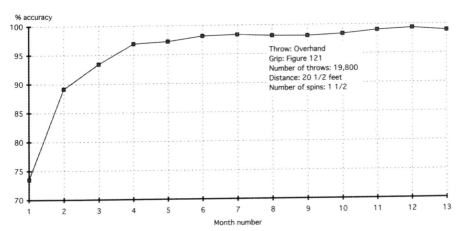

Figure 122. My sticking percentage for the ¹/₄" diameter, 7" long two-pointed flying sticker. To determine which end is hitting the target, I used orange tape on one end. I found this very helpful to check my consistency. The target is 10" wide x 12" tall.

5

Other Throwing Implements

Western dart

The Western dart is a very popular throwing implement. It is a light missile with an ingenious design.

Typically, a dart has a total length of 5" with a 2½" metal shaft with a needlelike tip. Attached (screwed) to it is a plastic tail with four vanes. The vanes function like the feathers of an arrow. They stabilize the dart in flight.

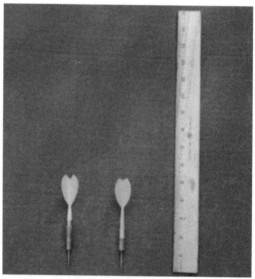

FIGURE 123. A Western dart. Some darts have shorter vanes than others. Longer vanes will have noticeable curves that could affect your throwing average.

GRIPPING A WESTERN DART

I use two grips on the dart. In one, I squeeze it with my thumb on one side and with the index, middle, and ring fingers at the opposite side (Figure 124A). In the other, I grip it only with my first three fingers (Figure 124B).

A   B

FIGURE 124. The four-finger (A) and three-finger (B) grips I use on a Western dart.

THROWING A WESTERN DART

It is not easy to throw an implement with no spin. However, at close distances the spin can be suppressed long enough until the implement hits the target. The most familiar no spin throwing implement is the spear. Still, the spear has to be held close to or at its CG to prevent it from spinning end over end. If the spear is gripped at the wrong location, it will still spin when thrown.

The very much shorter Japanese negishi-ryu shuriken can likewise be thrown with no spin. The spin is suppressed by applying downward pressure with the index finger (with the palm perpendicular to the ground) at the time of release. Additionally, horse or bear hair is attached to the tail of the negishi-ryu shuriken to stabilize it in flight and to prevent it from spinning.

The equally short Chinese flying dart can also be thrown with no spin. Its "Y" cross section makes it appear to have three vanes. However, because it is heavy, the vanes do not stabilize it in flight. The spin is suppressed by applying moderate pressure with the middle finger (by turning the palm down) at the time of release. Additionally, Chinese masters attach silk threads at its tail to stabilize it in flight and to prevent it from spinning.

The Japanese negishi-ryu shuriken and the Chinese flying dart have radically different shapes. Yet, if either is to be thrown with no spin, moderate pressure has to be applied at the time of release and/or there has to be a tail attachment.

On the other hand, it takes very little effort to throw a Western dart with no spin. Indeed, the no spin throw for a Western dart is effortless, thanks to the required attachment—the plastic tail with four vanes.

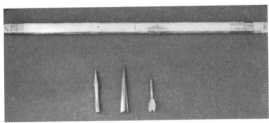

FIGURE 125. Implements I throw with no spin: top, the spear; bottom (left to right), a Japanese negishi-ryu shuriken, a Chinese flying dart, and a Western dart. A Chinese steel olive can also be thrown with no spin.

At close distances, the Western dart can be thrown with arm action only. However, from farther away, it has to be thrown like a knife where the twisting of the body reinforces the action of the arm. The arm action is very much like that in a baseball pitch.

It requires no effort to make a Western dart stick on the target. However, like other throwing implements, it has to be thrown with enough power to get to the target and with skill to hit what you are aiming at.

Damaged, loose, or curved vanes could affect your throwing average. To avoid damage to the vanes, use a maximum of five darts or use multiple targets (Figure 42). As an added precaution, when you hit the bull's-eye in your first throw, retrieve the dart immediately. From time to time, check to see if the vanes need to be tightened.

LEARNING CURVE CASE STUDY

A Western dart is normally thrown at a board that is partitioned in a number of ways. The throwing distance can be as close as 10 feet. Hence, throwing involves only the action of the arm.

There is no reason why a Western dart cannot be thrown from farther away. So I did.

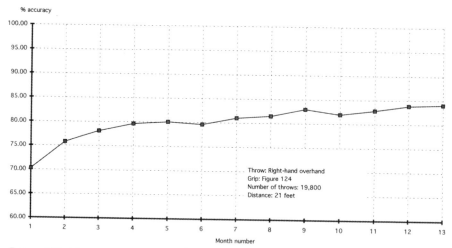

FIGURE 126. My percentage accuracy throwing a Western dart. The target is an 8¹/₂" x 11" sheet of paper.

Boomerang

Boomerangs are usually associated with Australian aborigines, although other peoples have also used them. There are two types of boomerangs: the returning, which is more of a plaything, and the non-returning, which is used in war.

The war boomerang or non-returning boomerang is designed to cut. They can be as long as 40 inches and sometimes even longer. This provides for the length of the fist with ample sharp length to cut a target with.

The returning boomerang is shorter—between 16 and 28 inches long. The arms are between 2" to 3" wide. The angle between the arms is between 70 and 120 degrees.

FIGURE 127. The steel one-way boomerangs I fabricated have two sharp tips, a pointed vertex, and dull edges. The boomerangs measure, from tip to tip, (left to right) 6¹/₄", 9¹/₂", and 10¹/₂". The angles between the arms are 90 degrees for the shorter boomerang and 120 degrees for the other two.

MAKING A BOOMERANG

I intended to throw a boomerang fifty times a day for thirteen months, so I had to make mine from steel plates. Wooden boomerangs will not withstand thirteen months of abuse.

I made three sizes of boomerangs from ¹/₈" thick steel plates (Figure 127). I kept the 1¹/₂" wide arms dull but departed from the usual design by giving my version of the boomerang sharp tips.

It is easy enough to hit the target with any part of the boomerang. However, I wanted to throw mine such that it would puncture the target. Hence, I kept the edges dull and made the tips sharp.

The hardwood arms of boomerangs thrown by Australian aborigines are skewed by 2- or 3-degrees from the coplanar. This and the special technique of throwing it makes the boomerang return to its thrower.

I did not want a pointed boomerang to return after being thrown. Hence, I kept the arms coplanar.

I coated one of the arms with fluorescent paint because I wanted to know which arm was sticking on the target.

GRIPPING A BOOMERANG

I use a knifelike grip on the boomerang (Figure 128) where I wrap my fingers around one of its arms.

THROWING A BOOMERANG

I throw a non-returning boomerang on a vertical and sometimes on a diagonal. Throwing one is like throwing a crooked knife or an ax.

It is more difficult to throw a 90-degree boomerang than a 120-degree boomerang. If the release of the 90-degree boomerang is not timed correctly, it will hook on the palm and hit low. To compensate for the hooking action, throw the 90-degree

FIGURE 128. The grip I use on a boomerang.

FIGURE 129. The boomerang is heavy and will impact a target with authority.

boomerang on an arc higher than you would throw the equivalent straight knife. There is little hooking action with the 120-degree boomerang.

The boomerang will hit the target in a number of ways: with its 2 sharp tips, with its corner tip like an arrow without a shaft, and with the outside of its two arms. The inside of the arms can also hit the target, particularly when the angle between the arms is 120 degrees.

LEARNING CURVE CASE STUDY

It will take more skill to get a boomerang to stick on the target than to get it to cut with its sharp edges. With a sharp-tipped boomerang, I was able to count my sticking percentage and generate a learning curve; you can do the same.

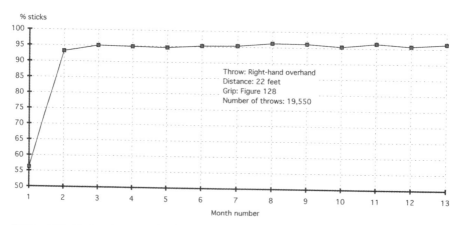

FIGURE 130. My learning curve for throwing a boomerang. I used a 90-degree boomerang in the first month and hit only 56 percent. From the second month on, I used the 120 degree 10^1/$_2$" boomerang at which time there was a marked improvement in my sticking average. The target is an 8^1/$_2$" x 11" rectangle.

6

Sport and Defensive Throwing

Skill will determine whether you will hit the target or not when throwing alone, in a sports competition, or in a defensive situation. However, in practice, the throwing distance is known; this is not so when you face an enemy who could be moving. So, a defensive throw must be quick and must be disguised by some ruse.

In sport knife throwing, the target is fixed. You would have marked your throwing distance with a line on the ground or with a short visible stake. For a particular throw and for a particular knife, you will be throwing from the same distance each time. If you miss the bull's-eye, your target will still be there the next day.

The requirements in sport knife throwing are more stringent. Your knife will have to stick on the target to get counted.

The desired effect of a defensive knife throw is also to make the knife stick on the target. However, even if a thrown knife hits flat or butt first, the throw would still "count." A throw that hits flat could still knock out the enemy. A throw that misses the nose but instead hits the eyes will inflict a more serious injury. A throw that merely grazes could make the enemy blink, thus, giving the thrower the time to make a getaway or to advance.

In sport knife throwing, you throw for points. In defensive knife throwing, you throw for keeps.

STICK FIGHTING, KNIFE FIGHTING, AND KNIFE THROWING

I consider knife throwing an integral part of stick and knife fighting. All stick and knife fighting techniques are throwing actions. For example: Strike downward with a stick. At the same time, open up your fingers. Do the same with a knife. The stick and the knife will fly away from your hands.

I had a student who attended stick and knife fighting classes for two years. In the twenty-third and twenty-fourth months, I decided that it was time for him to throw knives. I handed him my throwing knives and said, "Go ahead. Throw." His knives stuck. He was surprised, but I was not. Stick fighting and knife fighting prepared him for knife throwing.

WHY THROW AN IMPLEMENT?

Why should you throw a knife? If you miss, you would have lost your weapon.

Instinct will predispose a skilled thrower to pick up any object when there is a need for a defensive throw. The object that one could throw in a self-defense situation does not have to be a knife. It can be a can of sardines, a stone, an apple, or a tomato. Or a chair. Or sand. It is easier to hit a target with such objects because one need not be concerned about its orientation at contact. Any way a can of sardines hits, it is going to hurt—never mind a chair!

WHY LEARN MORE THAN ONE THROW?

For defensive knife throwing, you need to have more than one option. For example: Picture yourself in a situation where the adversary is crouched under a table. Your vertical or diagonal overhand throw will not get to him. Even a near-horizontal throw might not get to him. Similarly, outdoors, low tree branches will interfere with your overhand throw. Obviously, these situations require the use of an underhand throw.

However, if you were in knee-deep water or surrounded by knee-high reeds, you might not be able to throw underhand. You would be cutting water or grass with your throwing knife. In both instances, you have to throw overhand.

7

Throwing Implements and Your Hands

If you practice throwing only occasionally, you might take the care of your hands for granted. However, if you practice on a regular basis, your fingers can be rubbed raw by repeated throws. For this reason, the throwing implement must be (a) modified if needed and (b) kept clean, sharp, and repaired before and after use. The liberal use of duct tape will provide added protection. In winter, you will need to wear gloves.

Modifying the blade or the handle

Throwing implements such as knives, bagakays, axes, spears, shurikens, and shakens are not cheap. Some can also cut your fingers. For these reasons, you might need to modify them.

Doubled-edged throwing knives are designed to be thrown by the handle. If you want to throw them by the blade, the edges can be dulled on a bench grinder or by filing.

Knives with serrated backs, such as the AK-47 bayonet and the K-Bar can be thrown by the blade. Though the serration is not sharp, constant rubbing against your fingers at the time of release will cut your skin raw. To protect your hands, grind out the serration or put tape on it.

TAPING THE HANDLE

Taping the handle is almost necessary for knives that have plastic, rubber, or wooden scales. This will prevent the handle from chipping, or worse, splitting.

Taping is needed even more for the handle of the AK-47 bayonet. It is attached to a gun through deep grooves underneath its handle. To protect your hands, wrap the handle with two layers of duct tape. Make sure to tape the handle working toward the blade so that your fingers will not catch on the edges of the tape as you release the knife.

ADDING WEIGHT

You can increase the weight of a knife by wrapping several layers of duct tape on the handle. Of course, this will change the location of its CG and will change the behavior of the knife. I resort to this method to increase the weight of 4-ounce knives for throwing underhand.

MAKING THE IMPLEMENT MORE VISIBLE

Short lengths of orange electrical tape or a coat of fluorescent paint will make implements more visible when you throw on grass.

To avoid losing throwing implements, retrieve them immediately after a particularly bad throw. If you throw several more after a bad throw, you will not remember where to look for the errant implement. Also, if you do not retrieve it immediately, it will become mental clutter.

The most difficult weapons to find are the cigar-shaped steel bagakays, which can easily be lost in the grass. A metal detector is a good tool for finding lost knives, but a heavy magnet from a hardware store works just as well and costs under $20. It will literally suck up the lost knife. You would not want to mow your lawn with a lost knife in your yard!

Care of your throwing implements

Bring a fine file and a roll of duct tape to your throwing sessions.

The care of your throwing implements after use should become a matter of routine. It will extend their useful life, prevent cuts on your fingers, ensure many successful throws, and avoid the risk of a really bad throw.

If you hit an already embedded implement with another, retrieve both immediately. Run your fingers very lightly on them to check for nicks. Smooth any nick using a fine file, then remove any burr using sandpaper.

After you throw, clean all your implements with detergent to remove dirt, grass, or leaves. Apply the detergent with a sponge. Wipe the implement dry with a paper towel or a piece of cloth.

Check the tips for bends or chips. Hammer any bend using sharp, light taps over an anvil. Sharpen chipped tips with a file or on a bench grinder.

The wooden shaft of a spear will become chipped when hit by a subsequent throw. To prevent splinters from getting into your hands, smooth any chip with a file then put duct tape over it.

Many throwing implements, particularly knives, are made from stainless steel. However, there are many good throwing knives that are not rustproof. (You would be surprised at how fast some of these knives rust.) To remove thin layers of rust, use rust "erasers" which cost about $5. The axes, knives, bagakays, shurikens, shakens, flying darts, steel olives, and disks (coins) that I designed and fabricated are not rustproof. Hence, I put my rust "erasers" to good use.

Prevention is the best way of taking care of your throwing implements. To minimize the possibility of hitting an already embedded implement, I use a wide target that is 4-foot wide by 3-foot high. I partition this into smaller sections either by drawing a 12" wide by 14" tall rectangle or pasting images printed on 8½" by 11" paper on the target board. In this way, I am able to direct my subsequent throws to a still hole-free part of the board.

In precision throwing, when I hit the center of the target, I retrieve the implement immediately.

Care of your hands

If you throw a heavy all-metal ax, say, 100 times in one practice session everyday, the repeated throws will rub your thumb, index finger, and middle finger raw. To avoid losing your fingerprints, you can wrap two layers of duct tape on those fingers (Figure 131). One layer of duct tape wrapped around the handle of the ax will give you added protection. The duct tape on the handle, aside from protecting your skin, will also help prevent nicks on your ax. If you only throw occasionally, you will not need the duct tape.

You can also wrap the handles of your throwing knives with duct tape. However, you do not need to wrap tape on your fingers when you throw lighter throwing implements. You will experience a certain degree of discomfort in the beginning, but as you throw more, you will get used to the duct tape.

Eventually, abrasion will expose the glue and will make the duct tape sticky. When this happens retape the implement. If you do not have tape on hand, rub dirt on it—and clean it after practice.

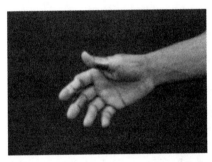

FIGURE 131. Duct tape on the index finger, thumb, and middle finger. Do not use more than two layers of duct tape. If you do, you will not be able to bend your fingers.

Conclusion: Art, Theory, and Practice

As mentioned in previous chapters there are many variables involved in a throw. These include

Physical
    Knife (or any implement)
    Grip
        Blade—there are a number of blade grips that can be used on a knife
        Handle—there are a number of handle grips that can be used on a knife
    Distance
    Type of throw: underhand or overhand
Physical, personal
    Physical condition
    Mechanics of the throw
Mental
    Mental clutter

If one is to make a knife stick, the number of *physical variables* must be kept to a minimum—ideally to zero. For example: One can throw ten identical knives, using the same grip, throwing from the same distance, and using the overhand throw. Thus, one has only two other variables to contend with: *physical (personal)* and *mental*.

You might be in good physical condition. Still, there are variables that could affect your throw. During the backward swing of your arm, you might inhale a lungful of exhaust fumes from a passing car. Of course, when you throw in a forest such a thing will not happen. Still, there could be mental clutter such as sound that breaks the silence or movement that suddenly appears in the corner of your eye.

In theory, if the thrower is to stick his knife when gripped by the blade, he should throw such that Equation 3 is satisfied.

$$\text{Throwing distance} = (2n + 1)Z + \text{Arm reach}$$

In practice, you can make a beginning thrower put his front toe on the exact spot for the throwing distance, you can give him a specific knife, and give him all sorts of instructions, but still he will not stick the knife consistently. If the beginner sticks the knife, it is more because of luck. Why?

There is more to the knife throw than meets the eye. There are variables that we cannot assign a number to and that do not show up in Equation 3.

We can represent a knife throw with a more complex equation that will determine not only throwing distance, but whether or not the knife will stick.

Good throw =
Must satisfy Equation 3
+ Zero physical variable
+ Zero mental clutter
+ Consistent (constant) mechanics of the throw

It is difficult not to have mental clutter when you throw. Lack of confidence is mental clutter. So are personal problems. However, with practice, the thrower can reduce mental clutter and can reach a mental state where he is able to "empty his mind"—where he is able to isolate his *self* from the rest of the universe.

You can keep records, compute your accuracy percentage, and generate a learning curve of your throws. In that way, you can measure your accuracy and express it with a number. On the other hand, one cannot assign a number to how "empty" the mind is nor can one assign a number to the consistency of the mechanics of his throw. These two variables are intricately linked—one cannot be separated from the other. However, art, a manifestation of this link, is observable.

Art, form, the smoothness of the throwing motion, results when the mechanics of the throw is mastered, when the mind is emptied—and when the knife sticks.

Epilogue: The Nail

I went to high school in Manila where my family had a small store. I would help at the store very early in the morning and after classes in the afternoon.

We sold grapes that were packed in sawdust inside wooden boxes. My father would open the box, pull out bunches of grapes and place them on the counter. Occasionally, there would be a grape or two that became detached from the bunch. I made a game of searching for them by touch in the sawdust. Those were the sweetest grapes I ever tasted.

Beyond the selling of grapes, my father also found use for the packing materials. The sawdust supplemented the wooden fuel that we cooked with. He would also pull out the nails from the wooden box and pile the wood neatly in a corner. He brought the bent nails home—for me to make straight. While I would have rather read books, I never complained about the chore. At the time, I did not realize that I was being given the *most important lesson of my life. I had to straighten the nails. I had to extract one more use from them.*

We sold a number of other things. Some we wrapped in old newspapers. However, *before the newspapers became wrappers, I read them and solved all the crossword puzzles I found.* Hence, I extracted one more use from the newspapers. I was able to make one more nail straight.

I could have concluded this book with the chapter "My Throwing Implements." Obviously, I didn't—because I had one more nail to make straight. I had to learn one more aspect of throwing. There was still part of my brain I had not used; there was still an arm movement I had not done; there was one more throw I had to learn so I added the chapter "Japanese Throwing Implements." To complete that chapter, I threw the shaken and the shuriken a total of 167,250 times.

I could not stop even then, though, as it didn't feel right to exclude Chinese throwing implements. I had one more nail to make straight, so I extended my self-imposed deadline. After 95,550 throws, I completed the chapter on Chinese throwing implements.

There were aches and pains along the way both physically and mentally. Over the fourteen years it took me to complete my goals, I experienced pain in my wrists, fingers, elbows, knees, ankles, soles, and toes. And head, too. Worst, there was a time when my eyes started going bad. I did not stop throwing my knives, though. I still kept score using the sound of the impact of the knife on my target to determine whether the knife hit point first or not. A knife that hits with its point first will make little noise—a dull thud. One that does not sounds, to me, like a thunderclap. Fortunately, after two eye operations, I have good eyesight again.

I threw the implements when it was very hot, when it was very cold, when there was snow on the ground, when it was drizzling, when I was sneezing, when I had a fever, when I was hobbling, when I was feeling lazy, and even when I had a heavy heart. I could have stopped but for one more nail.

I had planned to complete this work three chapters earlier, but I couldn't. There was still a grip I hadn't used and implements I hadn't thrown. I had to extract one more use from my arm. *It is a nail I had to make straight—one more time.*

Appendix A

Rules of competition for knife and ax throwing

These are the rules I use for my students. These rules are self-defense oriented since my students are allowed only a few tries to find their throwing distances.

The throwing area must be secured to ensure the safety of the competitors and spectators.

- **Throwing distance.** The throwing distance must be at least 16 feet. The contestant will be allowed three practice throws to determine his throwing distance. He will also be allowed to mark it.

- **Number of throws to qualify in the finals.** Each contestant will throw five consecutive times of which three must stick to qualify for the finals.

- **Number of throws in the finals.** Each contestant who qualifies for the finals will throw five times.

- **Target in the finals.** The target will consist of concentric circles with a maximum diameter of 8 inches and a minimum diameter of 2 inches.

- **The winner.** The winner will be the contestant with the most sticks.

In case of a tie, each contestant will be allowed one additional throw. The contestant who sticks his knife closest to the center of the target will be declared the winner.

Appendix B

Linear and angular speeds of a throwing implement

A point on a rotating object located at distance R from the axis of rotation traces a circle of radius R. For example: In knife throwing, the rotating object is the knife held in the hand, the point is any point in the knife such as its CG or its tip, and the axis of rotation is the thrower's shoulder.

The CG of the knife will have both linear speed (V) and angular speed (ω) which are defined as

$$V = \frac{\text{total distance traveled}}{\text{time interval}}$$

$$\omega = \frac{\text{angle traversed}}{\text{time interval}}$$

Angular speed (degrees/second or radians/second) is one of two ways to measure the rate of rotation. The other is angular frequency (f) which is defined as

$$f = \frac{\text{number of revolutions}}{\text{time interval}}$$

The unit of frequency (f) is revolutions/second or revolutions/minute.

Linear speed and angular speed are related by the equation

$$V = \omega R$$

which means that any point on the knife farther away from the shoulder will have a greater linear speed. Consider Figure 132.

The knife is held with its CG a distance r away from the shoulder. When released, it will have a linear speed of v, that is,

$$v = \omega r$$

If the knife is held such that its CG is farther away from the shoulder at a distance R, it will have a greater linear speed V (with ω held constant), that is,

$$V > v$$

For example: The CG of a shuriken held in the jikishin grip (Figure 88B) is closer to the axis of rotation (the shoulder joint) than when the shuriken is held as in Figure 91D. Thus, held as in Figure 91D, the shuriken when thrown will spin faster and will complete one full spin quicker. For this reason, for an equal number of spins, you will have to be farther from the target when you use Figure 88B than when you use Figure 91D.

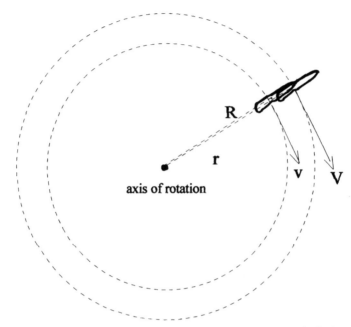

FIGURE 132. The center of the circle is the axis of rotation, which is the knife thrower's shoulder. (Not drawn to scale.)

References

Claude Blair, *The Complete Encyclopedia of Arms and Weapons*, Simon & Schuster, 1982, New York, New York.

Peter Brancazio, *Sport Science*, Simon & Schuster, 1984, New York, New York.

Douglas H. Y. Hsieh, *Ancient Chinese Hidden Weapons*, Meadea Enterprises Co., Inc., 1986, Republic of China.

Shirakami Ikku-ken, *Shuriken-Do*, Paul H. Crompton Ltd., 1987, London, England.

Amante P. Mariñas Sr., *Pananandata Guide to Knife Throwing*, United Cutlery Corp., 1999, Sevierville, Tennessee.

Harry K. McEvoy, *Knife Throwing A Practical Guide*, Charles E. Tuttle Company, Inc., 1973, Rutland, Vermont.

W. G. McLean and E. W. Nelson, *Schaum's Series Theory and Problems of Engineering Mechanics*, McGraw-Hill Book Company, 1988, New York, New York.

About the Author

Amante P. Mariñas, Sr., teaches pananandata, his family's fighting system, which he was introduced to when he was eight years old by his granduncle Ingkong Leon Marcelo. Mariñas holds black belts in shorin-ryu karate from the Commando Karate Club under Sensei Latino Gonzalez and Sensei Anselmo "Pop" Santos and in aikido from the Philippine Aikido Club under Sensei Ambrosio Gavileno.

He has written over 100 articles and is the world's most published practitioner of Filipino martial arts. He has authored nine other books including *Arnis de Mano, Arnis Lanada, Pananandata Knife Fighting, Pananandata Yantok at Daga, Pananandata Dalawang Yantok, Pananandata Rope Fighting, Pananandata Guide to Knife Throwing, Pananandata Guide to Sport Blowguns,* and *Pananandata: Its History and Techniques.*

Mariñas designed the VM Bulalakaw, which was marketed by United Cutlery Corporation. He has also designed and fabricated bagakays, other knives, axes, spears, and many-pointed throwing implements.

Mariñas is originally from Pambuan, a small village in Gapan, Nueva Ecija, in Central Luzon in the Philippines. He taught chemical engineering at Adamson University in Manila before coming to the United States. Today he lives in Fredericksburg, Virginia, with his wife, Cherry. His son, Amante Jr., is heir to pananandata.